BLOCKC
DESIG &
USE CASES

Parveen A.

Associate Professor,
Dept of CSE, Sathyabama Institute
of Science and Technology

KHANNA BOOK
PUBLISHING CO. (P) Ltd.
4C/4344, Ansari Road, Darya Ganj,
New Delhi, India

Sathyabama Institute of
Science and Technology
Jeppiaar Nagar, Rajiv Gandhi Salai,
Chennai, Tamilnadu, India

Dear Readers,

To prevent the piracy, this book is secured with HIGH SECURITY HOLOGRAM on the front title cover. In case you don't find the hologram on the front cover title, please write us to at contact@khannabooks.com or whatsapp us at +91-99109 09320 and avail special gift voucher for yourself.

Specimen of Hologram on front Cover title:

Moreover, there is a SPECIAL DISCOUNT COUPON for you with EVERY HOLOGRAM.

How to avail this SPECIAL DISCOUNT:

Step 1: Scratch the hologram
Step 2: Under the scratch area, your "coupon code" is available
Step 3: Logon to www.khannabooks.com
Step 4: Use your "coupon code" in the shopping cart and get your copy at a special discount
Step 5: Enjoy your reading!

Thanks,
Khanna Publishing House

ISBN: 978-93-55384-02-7

BLOCKCHAIN AND USE CASES
by **Parveen A.**

First Edition: 2025

To view complete list of books, please scan the QR Code:

Published by:
Khanna Book Publishing Co. (P) Ltd.
CIN: U22110DL1998PTC095547

Visit us at: www.khannabooks.com
Write us at: contact@khannabooks.com

Printed in Bharat.

Preface

"Blockchain Design and Use Cases" is your guide to mastering blockchain technology, starting with its foundational primitives and architectural frameworks. We explore how consensus mechanisms drive integrity, then dive into practical applications like KYC and financial blockchains, highlighting their revolutionary potential.

This book equips you with the knowledge to design robust systems using Hyperledger Fabric A & B, create effective privacy policies, and implement cryptographic schemes, ensuring you're ready to navigate and innovate in the rapidly evolving blockchainscenarios.

Contents

UNIT 1

Introduction to Blockchain

RATIONALE

Unit 1 is foundational to understanding blockchain technology, as it introduces the core concepts and architecture that underpin the system. It explains the transition from digital money to distributed ledgers, the design principles such as security, consensus, and privacy, and the cryptographic primitives like hashes and digital signatures that ensure data integrity. By covering the evolution from hashchains to blockchains and exploring basic consensus mechanisms, this unit equips readers with the essential knowledge needed to comprehend more advanced topics. It lays a strong groundwork for understanding blockchain's technical structure and its potential applications across industries.

OUTCOMES

- Understand the evolution of blockchain technology, from digital money to distributed ledgers, and its foundational design principles such as security, consensus, permissions, and privacy.
- Gain knowledge of blockchain architecture and cryptographic primitives like hashing and digital signatures, which ensure data integrity and security.
- Comprehend the transition from hashchains to blockchains and explore basic consensus mechanisms that enable decentralized decision-making.
- Develop the ability to analyze blockchain systems and their components, providing a solid foundation for advanced topics and practical applications.

1.1 DIGITAL MONEY TO DISTRIBUTED LEDGERS

1.1.1 Introduction to Digital Money

Digital money, also known as electronic currency or digital currency, refers to any form of currency that is available only in digital form and not in physical form. It encompasses a wide range of financial instruments, including cryptocurrencies like Bitcoin, stablecoins, and central bank digital currencies (CBDCs). The rise of digital money has been closely linked to the evolution of technology and the internet, which have transformed how transactions are conducted globally.

The introduction of Bitcoin in 2009 by an anonymous entity known as Satoshi Nakamoto marked a significant milestone in the history of digital money. Bitcoin was the first decentralized cryptocurrency that utilized blockchain technology to enable peer-to-peer transactions without the need for intermediaries such as banks. This innovation sparked a revolution in the financial sector and led to the development of thousands of alternative cryptocurrencies.

1.1.2 The Evolution of Distributed Ledger Technology (DLT)

Distributed Ledger Technology (DLT) is a foundational technology that underpins digital currencies. DLT refers to a decentralized database that is shared across multiple locations or among multiple participants. Each participant has access to the same information, ensuring transparency and reducing the risk of fraud. Unlike traditional databases controlled by a central authority, DLT as in figure 1.1operates on a peer-to-peer network where each node can validate and record transactions.

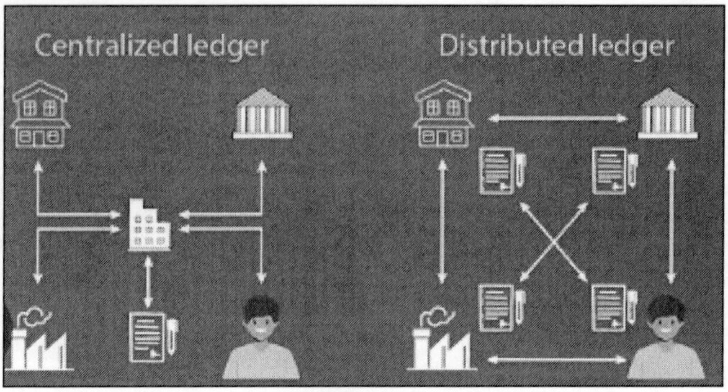

Figure 1.1: *DLT*

The evolution of DLT can be traced back to early concepts of distributed systems but gained significant traction with the advent of blockchain technology. Blockchain is a specific type of DLT that organizes data into blocks linked together in chronological order, creating an immutable chain. This structure enhances security and trust among participants, making it particularly suitable for financial transactions. The properties of DLT is as given in figure 1.2.

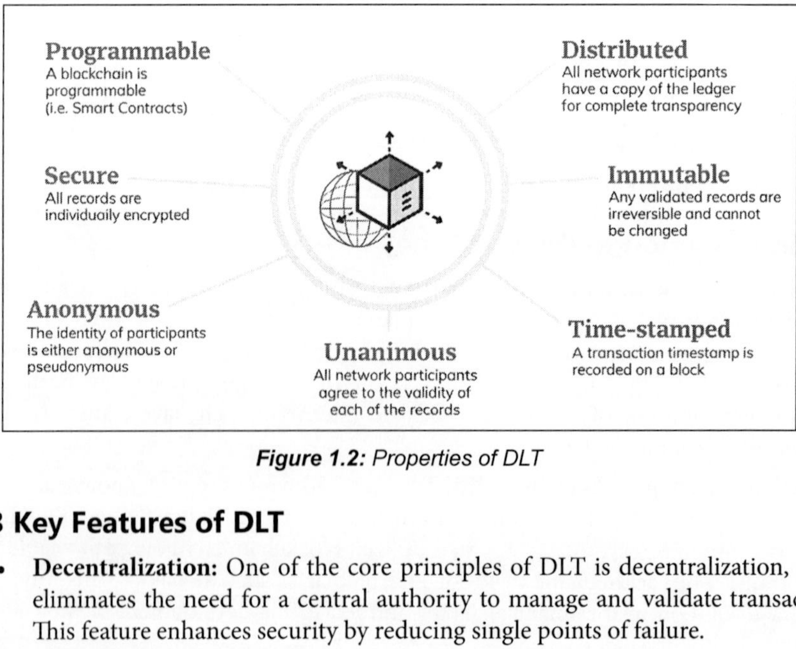

Figure 1.2: *Properties of DLT*

1.1.3 Key Features of DLT

- **Decentralization:** One of the core principles of DLT is decentralization, which eliminates the need for a central authority to manage and validate transactions. This feature enhances security by reducing single points of failure.

- **Transparency:** All participants in a DLT network have access to the same information, promoting transparency and trust. Transactions are recorded in real-time, allowing participants to verify their authenticity.
- **Immutability:** Once data is recorded on a distributed ledger, it cannot be altered or deleted without consensus from the network participants. This immutability feature protects against fraud and unauthorized changes.
- **Security:** DLT employs cryptographic techniques to secure data and ensure that only authorized users can access or modify it. Each transaction is digitally signed, providing an additional layer of security.
- **Efficiency:** By streamlining processes and reducing reliance on intermediaries, DLT can significantly enhance transaction speeds and reduce costs associated with traditional banking systems.

1.1.4 Applications of DLT in Digital Money

The applications of DLT extend beyond cryptocurrencies; they have been adopted across various sectors.

- **Financial Services:** Banks and financial institutions are increasingly exploring DLT for cross-border payments, trade finance, and clearing and settlement processes. The technology enables faster transactions while reducing costs associated with traditional banking systems.
- **Supply Chain Management:** DLT enhances transparency and traceability in supply chains by providing real-time visibility into product movements from manufacturers to consumers. Companies can track goods at every stage, reducing fraud and improving accountability.
- **Healthcare:** In healthcare, DLT can securely store patient records while ensuring privacy and compliance with regulations such as HIPAA. Patients can control access to their data while allowing healthcare providers to share information seamlessly.
- **Voting Systems:** Blockchain-based voting systems have been proposed as a way to enhance electoral transparency and reduce fraud. Voters can cast their votes securely while ensuring that results are verifiable.

The transition from traditional forms of money to digital currencies facilitated by distributed ledger technology represents a paradigm shift in how value is exchanged globally. As organizations continue to explore innovative applications for DLT, its potential impact on various industries will likely expand further, reshaping the future landscape of finance and beyond.

Video Resources
https://www.youtube.com/watch?v=Cqk7PN8f8gM

Use of ICT

https://www.geeksforgeeks.org/blockchain-and-distributed-ledger-technology-dlt/

Applications (Real Life/Industrial)

1. Singapore and Canada

The Monetary Authority of Singapore (MAS) and the Bank of Canada (BOC) conducted experiments linking their domestic payment systems using Distributed Ledger Technology

(DLT). This enabled cross-border payments and settlements using central bank digital currencies (CBDCs) without intermediaries.

2. China

China has implemented its Central Bank Digital Currency (CBDC), the Digital Yuan (eCNY), which is supported by blockchain technology. It is used domestically for retail payments and is being tested for cross-border transactions to enhance efficiency and financial inclusion.

3. European Union and Japan

The European Central Bank (ECB) and the Bank of Japan have explored DLT for securities settlement projects under initiatives like Project Stella, which aims to improve the efficiency of cross-border payments and settlements.

These examples highlight how countries are leveraging DLT to transform payment systems, reduce costs, and enhance transparency in financial transactions.

Case-Study (Environmental/Sustainability / Social/Ethical Issues)

The adoption of digital money and distributed ledger technology (DLT) offers significant benefits, such as transparency, efficiency, and cost reduction. However, these technologies also raise environmental and ethical concerns that need to be addressed for sustainable implementation.

Environmental Issues: Energy Consumption

Case Example: Bitcoin Mining

Bitcoin, which operates on blockchain (a type of DLT), requires significant computational power to validate transactions through a process called mining. This process consumes vast amounts of electricity, often sourced from non-renewable energy.

According to studies, Bitcoin's annual energy consumption rivals that of small countries like Argentina, contributing to carbon emissions and environmental degradation.

Impact

The high energy demand raises concerns about the sustainability of blockchain-based systems if renewable energy sources are not prioritized.

Social and Ethical Issues: Financial Inclusion vs. Inequality

Case Example: Central Bank Digital Currencies (CBDCs) in Developing Countries

While CBDCs aim to promote financial inclusion by providing banking access to unbanked populations, they also risk exacerbating inequality if digital infrastructure is unevenly distributed. For instance, in countries with limited internet access or low smartphone penetration, rural or marginalized communities may struggle to adopt digital currencies, creating a digital divide.

Impact

Ethical concerns arise regarding equitable access to these technologies and the potential exclusion of vulnerable populations.

Ethical Concerns: Privacy and Surveillance

Case Example: China's Digital Yuan (eCNY)

The Digital Yuan, issued by the Chinese government, leverages DLT for secure transactions but raises ethical questions about privacy. The centralized nature of the system allows the government to monitor transactions in real time.

Impact

This level of surveillance can lead to misuse of data, erosion of individual privacy, and potential suppression of dissent.

Sustainability Solutions

- Transitioning blockchain systems to renewable energy sources can reduce their environmental footprint.
- Governments and organizations must ensure equitable access to digital infrastructure to prevent social exclusion.
- Privacy-preserving technologies like zero-knowledge proofs can address ethical concerns while maintaining transparency.

This case study highlights the need for balancing technological innovation with environmental sustainability and ethical considerations for widespread adoption of digital money and distributed ledgers.

Create Inquisitiveness and Curiosity

The integration of digital money with distributed ledger technology (DLT) has sparked both excitement and concern. On one hand, DLT offers transformative benefits like transparency, efficiency, and financial inclusion. However, it also raises ethical and social issues.

For instance, China's Digital Yuan (eCNY) allows real-time transaction monitoring, raising privacy concerns and potential misuse for surveillance. Similarly, while CBDCs in developing nations aim to include unbanked populations, they risk exacerbating inequality if digital infrastructure and literacy are not adequately developed.

To address these challenges, solutions like privacy-preserving technologies, infrastructure development, and ethical frameworks are crucial. This balance between innovation and responsibility will determine whether these technologies enhance or hinder societal progress.

Solved Problems (With increasing difficulty level)

Beginner Level

Problem 1: Understanding Digital Money

- **Scenario**: Alice wants to send $100 to Bob using digital money. Explain how digital money works and how the transaction is processed using distributed ledger technology (DLT).
- **Solution**: Digital money represents fiat currency in electronic form. Alice initiates the transfer using a digital wallet. The transaction is recorded on a distributed ledger, where multiple nodes validate it using a consensus mechanism. Once validated, the ledger updates across all nodes, ensuring transparency and security.

Intermediate Level

Problem 2: Cross-Border Payment Efficiency

- **Scenario**: A company in Singapore wants to pay a supplier in Canada using a blockchain-based platform. Compare this process with traditional banking methods.
- **Solution**: In traditional banking, cross-border payments involve intermediaries like correspondent banks, leading to delays and high fees. Using blockchain (a type of DLT), the transaction is processed directly between parties, validated by nodes on the network, and settled almost instantly. This reduces costs, eliminates intermediaries, and ensures transparency.

Advanced Level

Problem 3: Smart Contracts for Supply Chain

- **Scenario**: A retailer uses smart contracts on a distributed ledger to automate payments to suppliers once goods are delivered. How does this system work, and what are its advantages?
- **Solution**: The retailer creates a smart contract specifying payment terms (e.g., payment is released when goods are delivered). When the delivery is confirmed (via IoT devices or manual input), the smart contract automatically executes the payment. Advantages include reduced manual intervention, faster processing, and minimized disputes due to transparent records on the ledger.

These problems progress in complexity, helping learners understand the practical applications of digital money and distributed ledgers in real-world scenarios.

1.2 DESIGN PRIMITIVES: PROTOCOLS, SECURITY, CONSENSUS, PERMISSIONS, PRIVACY

1.2.1 Introduction to Design Primitives

In the context of distributed ledger technology (DLT) and blockchain systems, design primitives refer to fundamental building blocks that underpin the architecture and functionality of these technologies. These primitives include protocols for communication between nodes, security mechanisms for protecting data integrity, consensus algorithms for agreement among participants, permissions for access control, and privacy measures for safeguarding sensitive information.

1.2.2 Protocols

Protocols define the rules governing communication between nodes in a distributed network. They specify how data is transmitted, validated, and recorded on the ledger. Common protocols used in blockchain networks include the following.

Peer-to-Peer (P2P) Protocols

These protocols enable direct communication between nodes without relying on intermediaries. P2P protocols as in figure 1.3, facilitate efficient data sharing and transaction validation across the network.

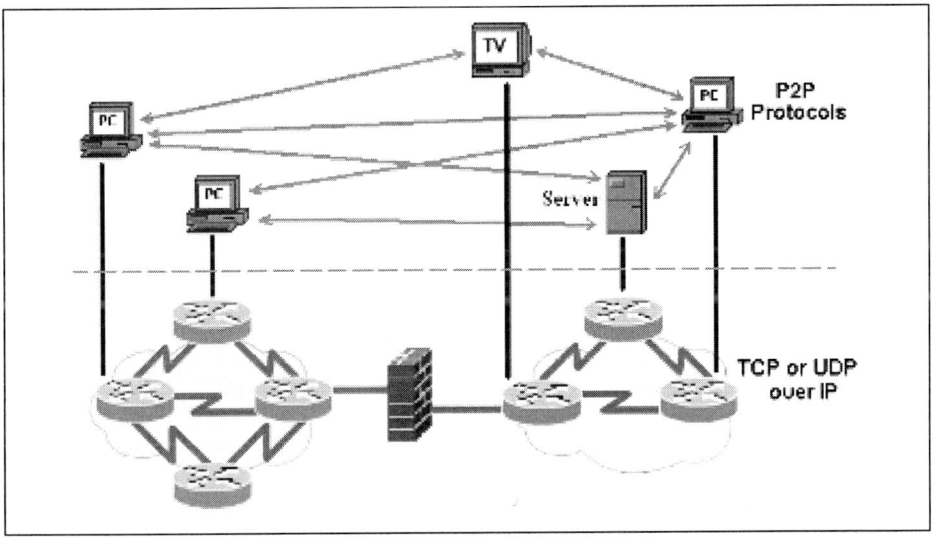

Figure 1.3: *Peer to Peer Network Protocols*

Transaction Protocols

Transaction protocols as in figure 1.4, outline how transactions are created, signed, broadcasted, validated, and recorded on the ledger. They ensure that all nodes follow consistent procedures when processing transactions.

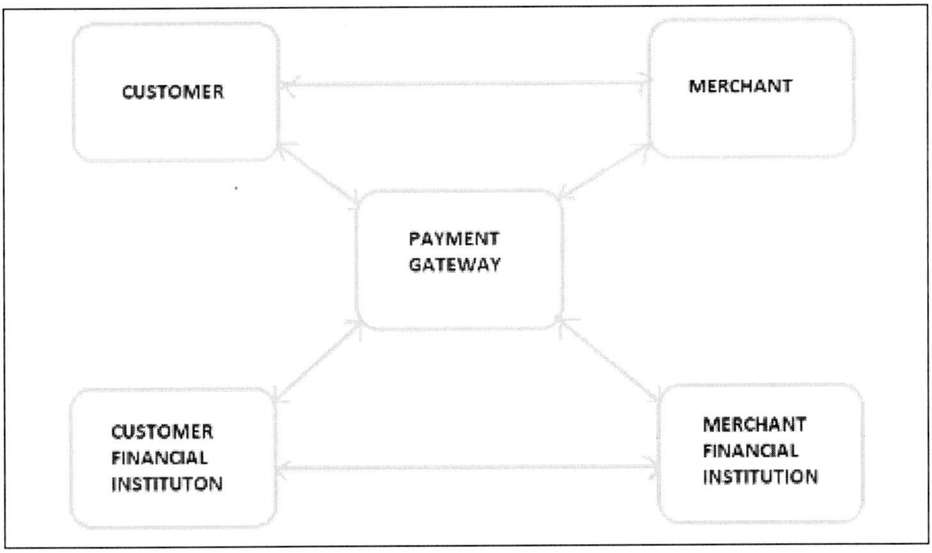

Figure 1.4: *Secure Electronic Transaction Protocol*

Smart Contract Protocols

Smart contracts as given in figure 1.5, are self-executing contracts with terms directly written into code. Protocols governing smart contracts define how they are deployed, executed, and interacted with on the blockchain.

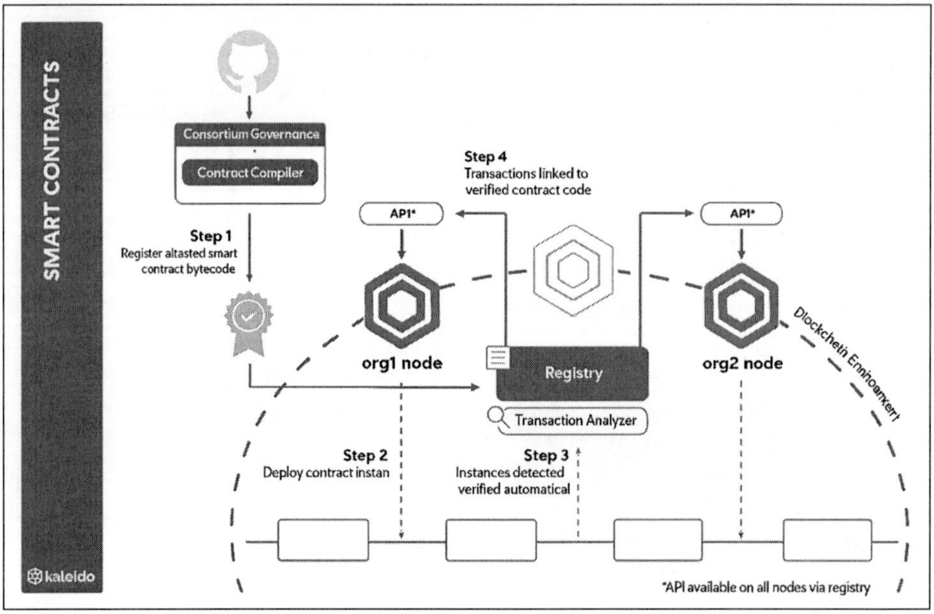

Figure 1.5: *Smart Contracts*

1.2.3 Security

Security is paramount in distributed ledger systems due to their decentralized nature and exposure to potential threats.

- **Cryptographic Techniques**: Cryptography secures data through encryption methods that protect transaction details from unauthorized access or tampering. Public-key cryptography enables users to generate unique keys for signing transactions securely.
- **Digital Signatures**: Digital signatures authenticate transactions by verifying the identity of the sender using their private key while allowing others to validate it using their public key.
- **HashFunctions**: Hash functions convert input data into fixed-length strings (hashes) that uniquely represent that data. Hashing ensures data integrity by enabling users to verify whether any changes have occurred since it was recorded on the ledger.

1.2.4 Consensus Mechanisms

Consensus mechanisms are critical for achieving agreement among distributed nodes regarding the state of the ledger:

- **Proof of Work (PoW):** In PoW systems like Bitcoin, miners compete to solve complex mathematical problems as proof of their computational effort before validating transactions and creating new blocks.
- **Proof of Stake (PoS):** PoS allows validators to create new blocks based on their stake or ownership in the cryptocurrency rather than computational power—encouraging energy efficiency compared to PoW models.

- **Delegated Proof of Stake (DPoS):** In DPoS systems like EOSIO, stakeholders elect delegates who validate transactions on their behalf—improving scalability while maintaining decentralization.
- **Practical Byzantine Fault Tolerance (PBFT):** PBFT is designed for permissioned networks where nodes must reach consensus even if some participants act maliciously or fail—ensuring reliability in critical applications.

1.2.5 Permissions

Permissions govern who can participate in a distributed ledger network.

- **Public vs Private Networks:** Public blockchains allow anyone to join and participate freely (e.g., Bitcoin), while private blockchains restrict access only to authorized entities—providing greater control over participation levels as given in figure 1.6.

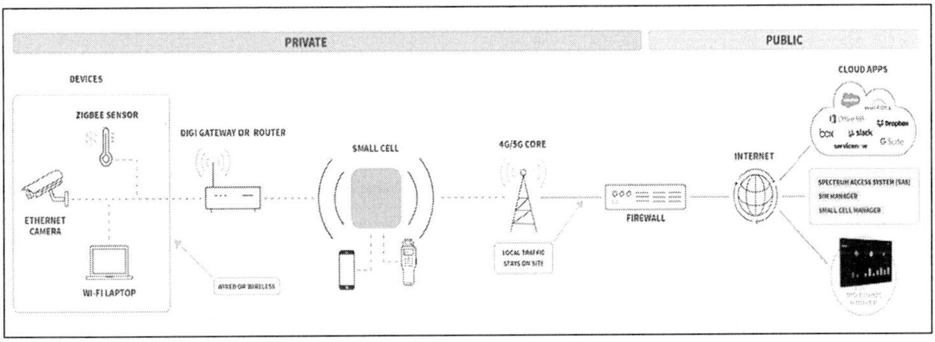

Figure 1.6: *Public vs. Private Networks*

- **Role-Based Access Control (RBAC):** RBAC assigns permissions based on user roles within an organization—ensuring that only authorized personnel can perform specific actions within the network.
- **Identity Management:** Identity management solutions verify user identities before granting them access rights—enhancing security while maintaining accountability within permissioned networks.

1.2.6 Privacy Measures

Privacy measures protect sensitive information within distributed ledgers.

- **Zero-Knowledge Proofs (ZKPs):** ZKPs allow one party to prove knowledge about certain information without revealing that information itself—enabling privacy-preserving transactions on public blockchains.
- **Confidential Transactions:** Confidential transaction protocols encrypt transaction amounts while still allowing validation by network participants—ensuring privacy without compromising security or auditability.
- **Data Masking Techniques:** Data masking techniques obfuscate sensitive information stored on ledgers—allowing organizations to comply with regulations while maintaining operational efficiency.

Design primitives such as protocols, security mechanisms, consensus algorithms, permissions frameworks, and privacy measures play crucial roles in shaping distributed ledger technologies' architecture and functionality. By understanding these foundational elements better; developers can create more robust solutions tailored specifically toward meeting user needs while addressing challenges present within existing systems effectively moving forward!

Video Resources
https://www.youtube.com/watch?v=-mWjDgVWI20

Use of ICT

ICT tools like Hyperledger Fabric, Multichain, Enterprise Ethereum, Corda, and Quorum can be used to implement different blockchain protocols, each tailored for specific use cases and industries.

Applications (Real Life / Industrial)

- **Healthcare:** Blockchain is used to securely store medical records, ensuring privacy and integrity.
- **Media:** Blockchain-based platforms like DTube use decentralized networks for content sharing, enhancing transparency and fairness.
- **Government:** Blockchain is used to enhance transparency in government operations and ensure secure voting systems.

Case-Study (Environmental/Sustainability/Social/Ethical Issues)

IBM's blockchain water management system in California is a compelling case study that highlights the application of design primitives—protocols, security, consensus, permissions, and privacy—in addressing environmental sustainability and social/ethical issues. The system utilizes blockchain protocols to ensure transparent and secure recording of water allocation transactions, leveraging cryptographic primitives for data security and tamper-proofing.

A consensus mechanism, possibly a permissioned blockchain like Hyperledger Fabric, ensures collective agreement among stakeholders on water allocation decisions. The system is permissioned, allowing only authorized entities to access and influence water management, while privacy-enhancing technologies protect sensitive user data. This initiative promotes environmental sustainability by conserving water resources during droughts and supports equitable distribution, reducing conflicts over this vital resource. By empowering local communities with transparent access to water resources, the system also addresses social and ethical concerns, demonstrating how blockchain's design primitives can contribute to sustainable resource management and community empowerment.

Create Inquisitiveness and Curiosity

Blockchain technology's design primitivesprotocols, security, consensus, permissions, and privacy hold the key to unlocking a more efficient and secure digital future. By leveraging advanced blockchain protocols, we can create seamless interoperability between different networks, revolutionizing cross-chain transactions and fostering a more connected ecosystem.

Enhanced cryptographic primitives can fortify blockchain security, safeguarding it against even the most sophisticated threats. Novel consensus mechanisms can optimize both security and scalability, solving the long-standing trade-off between these critical factors. Permissioned blockchains can be designed to balance privacy with transparency, protecting sensitive data while allowing necessary oversight.

Furthermore, integrating privacy-enhancing technologies like zero-knowledge proofs into mainstream applications can ensure that user privacy is protected, making private transactions the norm. These advancements not only address current challenges but also open up new possibilities for blockchain technology to transform industries and improve lives.

Solved Problems (With Increasing Difficulty Level)

Problem 1: Basic Understanding of Blockchain Protocols

- **Problem Statement**: Explain how blockchain protocols ensure data integrity and transparency.
- **Solution**: Blockchain protocols use cryptographic primitives like hash functions to ensure that data is tamper-proof. Each block contains a unique hash that links it to the previous block, creating a chain that prevents data modification without detection.

Problem 2: Security through Cryptographic Primitives

- **Problem Statement**: Describe how digital signatures enhance security in blockchain transactions.
- **Solution**: Digital signatures, such as those using ECDSA, ensure that transactions are authentic and non-repudiable. A sender signs a transaction with their private key, which can be verified by others using the sender's public key, ensuring that only the sender could have initiated the transaction.

Problem 3: Consensus Mechanisms

- **Problem Statement**: Compare Proof-of-Work (PoW) and Proof-of-Stake (PoS) consensus algorithms in terms of energy efficiency and security.
- **Solution**: PoW is energy-intensive and secure but slow, while PoS is more energy-efficient and faster but less secure against certain attacks. PoW requires significant computational power to solve complex puzzles, whereas PoS relies on validators "staking" their own coins to validate transactions4.

Problem 4: Permissions and Access Control

- **Problem Statement**: Design a permissioned blockchain system for a healthcare network.
- **Solution**: Implement a permissioned blockchain using Hyperledger Fabric, where access is restricted to authorized healthcare providers. Use role-based access control (RBAC) to ensure that only specific personnel can view or modify patient records, enhancing privacy and security.

Problem 5: Privacy Enhancements

- **Problem Statement**: Explain how zero-knowledge proofs can enhance privacy in blockchain transactions.

- **Solution**: Zero-knowledge proofs allow users to prove that a statement is true without revealing any underlying information. In blockchain, this means that transactions can be verified as valid without exposing the transaction details, ensuring privacy while maintaining network trust.

Problem 6: Advanced Privacy and Security

- **Problem Statement**: Develop a blockchain system that integrates both homomorphic encryption and zero-knowledge proofs for enhanced privacy.
- **Solution**: Design a system where transactions are encrypted using homomorphic encryption, allowing computations to be performed on encrypted data. Additionally, use zero-knowledge proofs to verify the validity of transactions without revealing any sensitive information. This combination ensures both privacy and security in complex computations.

Problem 7: Scalability and Consensus

- **Problem Statement**: Propose a solution to improve the scalability of blockchain while maintaining security using a novel consensus algorithm.
- **Solution**: Develop a consensus algorithm that combines elements of PoS with sharding, allowing the network to process multiple transactions in parallel. This approach can significantly increase transaction throughput while maintaining the security benefits of a decentralized network.

Problem 8: Interoperability and Protocols

- **Problem Statement**: Design a protocol for interoperability between different blockchain networks.
- **Solution**: Implement a cross-chain protocol that enables seamless asset transfer between networks. Use a combination of hash locking and smart contracts to ensure that transactions are atomic and secure across different blockchain architectures.

Each problem builds upon the concepts of blockchain design primitives, increasing in complexity and requiring a deeper understanding of how these primitives interact to solve real-world challenges.

1.3 BLOCKCHAIN ARCHITECTURE AND DESIGN

1.3.1 Introduction to Design Primitives

A Blockchain is a distributed journal where all parties hold a local copy. However, based on the type of blockchain structure and its context, the system can be more centralized or decentralized. This simply refers to the blockchain architecture design and who controls the ledger.

Blockchain architecture as given in figure 1.7 refers to the structural design that defines how blockchain networks operateincluding components like nodes (participants), consensus mechanisms (validation processes), cryptographic primitives (security measures), smart contracts (automated agreements), etc., all working together cohesively towards achieving common goals within decentralized ecosystems effectively.

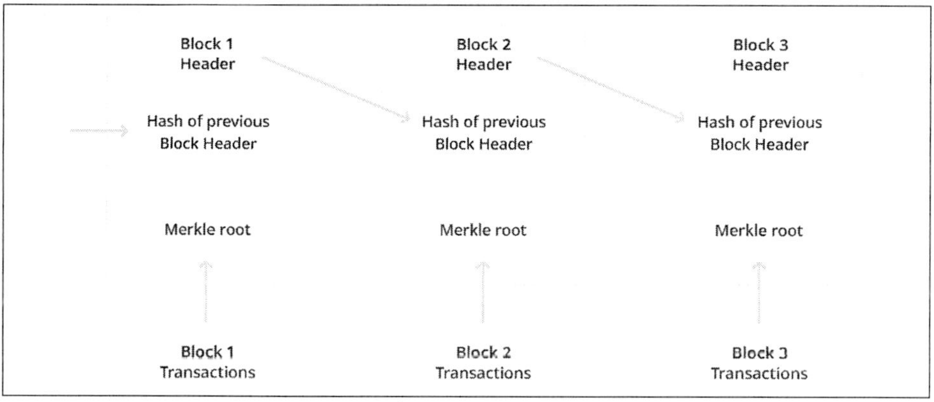

Figure 1.7: *Blockchain Structure*

These are the core blockchain architecture components:

- **Node:** user or computer within the blockchain architecture (each has an independent copy of the whole blockchain ledger).
- **Transaction:** smallest building block of a blockchain system (records, information, etc.) that serves as the purpose of blockchain.
- **Block:** a data structure used for keeping a set of transactions which is distributed to all nodes in the network.
- **Chain:** a sequence of blocks in a specific order.
- **Miners:** specific nodes which perform the block verification process before adding anything to the blockchain structure.
- **Consensus (consensus protocol):** a set of rules and arrangements to carry out blockchain operations

Any new record or transaction within the blockchain implies the building of a new block. Each record is then proven and digitally signed to ensure its genuineness. Before this block is added to the network, it should be verified by the majority of nodes in the system.

Figure 1.8 is a blockchain architecture diagram that shows how this actually works in the form of a digital wallet.

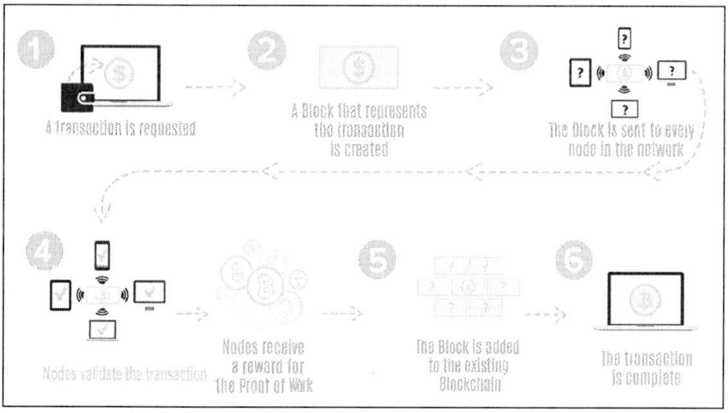

Figure 1.8: *How Blockchain Works*

Let's have a closer look at what is a block in a blockchain. Each blockchain block consists of:

- certain data
- the hash of the block
- the hash from the previous block

The data stored inside each block depends on the type of blockchain. For instance, in the Bitcoin blockchain structure, the block maintains data about the receiver, sender, and the amount of coins.

A hash is like a fingerprint (long record consisting of some digits and letters). Each block hash is generated with the help of a cryptographic hash algorithm (SHA 256). Consequently, this helps to identify each block in a blockchain structure easily. The moment a block is created, it automatically attaches a hash, while any changes made in a block affect the change of a hash too. Simply stated, hashes help to detect any changes in blocks.

The final element within the block is the hash from a previous block. This creates a chain of blocks and is the main element behind blockchain architecture's security. As an example, block 45 points to block 46. The very first block in a chain is a bit special - all confirmed and validated blocks are derived from the genesis block.

Any corrupt attempts provoke the blocks to change. All the following blocks then carry incorrect information and render the whole blockchain system invalid.

On the other hand, in theory, it could be possible to adjust all the blocks with the help of strong computer processors. However, there is a solution that eliminates this possibility called proof-of-work.

This allows a user to slow down the process of creation of new blocks. In Bitcoin blockchain architecture, it takes around 10 minutes to determine the necessary proof-of-work and add a new block to the chain. This work is done by miners - special nodes within the Bitcoin blockchain structure. Miners get to keep the transaction fees from the block that they verified as a reward.

Each new user (node) joining the peer-to-peer network of blockchain receives a full copy of the system. Once a new block is created, it is sent to each node within the blockchain system. Then, each node verifies the block and checks whether the information stated there is correct. If everything is alright, the block is added to the local blockchain in each node.

All the nodes inside a blockchain architecture create a consensus protocol. A consensus system is a set of network rules, and if everyone abides by them, they become self-enforced inside the blockchain.

For example, the Bitcoin blockchain has a consensus rule stating that a transaction amount must be cut in half after every 200,000 blocks. This means that if a block produces a verification reward of 10 BTC, this value must be halved after every 200,000 blocks.

As well, there can only be 4 million BTC left to be mined, since there is a maximum of 21 million BTC laid down in the Bitcoin blockchain system by the protocol. Once the miners unlock this many, the supply of Bitcoins ends unless the protocol is changed.

To recap, this makes blockchain technology immutable and cryptographically secure by eliminating any third-parties. It is impossible to tamper with the blockchain system; as it would be necessary to tamper with all of its blocks, recalculate the proof-of-work for each block, and also control more than 50% of all the nodes in a peer-to-peer network.

All blockchain structures fall into three categories as shown in figure 1.9.

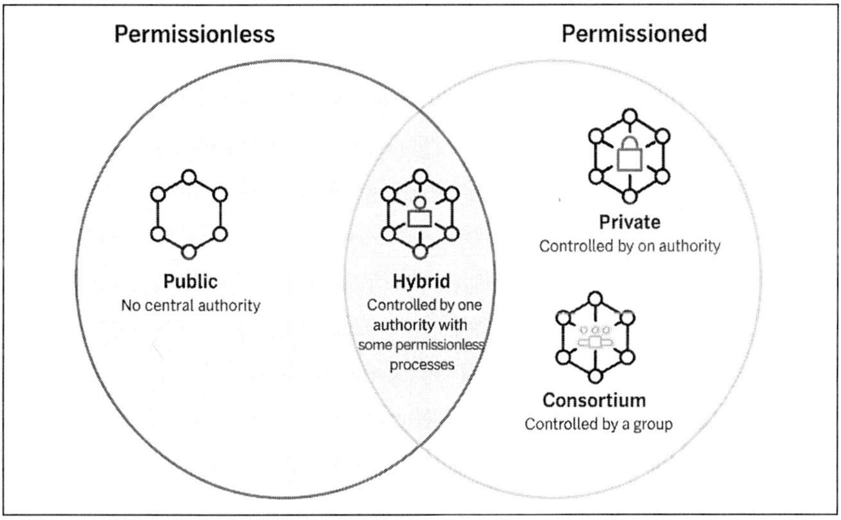

Figure 1.9: *Types of Blockchain Architecture*

1.3.2.1 Public Blockchain Architecture

A public blockchain architecture means that the data and access to the system is available to anyone who is willing to participate (e.g. Bitcoin, Ethereum, and Litecoin blockchain systems are public).In a public blockchain, all records are visible to the public and anyone could take part in the agreement process. On the other hand, this is less efficient since it takes a considerable amount of time to accept each new record into the blockchain architecture. On the contrary, a public blockchain is open-ended and thus decentralized.

1.3.2.2 Private Blockchain Architecture

As opposed to public blockchain architecture, the private system is controlled only by users from a specific organization or authorized users who have an invitation for participation.A private blockchain is considered more centralized since it is controlled by a particular group with increased privacy.

1.3.2.3 Consortium Blockchain Architecture

This blockchain structure can consist of a few organizations. In a consortium, procedures are set up and controlled by the preliminary assigned users.

The following table 1 provides a detailed comparison among these three blockchain systems.

Table 1.1: *Comparison among three blockchain systems*

Property	Public blockchain	Consortium blockchain	Private blockchain
Consensus determination	All miners	Selected set of nodes	Within one organization
Read permission	Public	Public or restricted	Public or restricted

Property	Public blockchain	Consortium blockchain	Private blockchain
Immutability level	Almost impossible to tamper	Could be tampered	Could be tampered
Efficiency (use of resources)	Low	High	High
Centralization	No	Partial	Yes
Consensus process	Permissionless	Needs permission	Needs permission

Video Resources

1. Blockchain Solution Architecture Specialization
   https://www.coursera.org/specializations/blockchain-solution-architecture
2. Fundamentals of Blockchain Architecture
   https://www.coursera.org/learn/fundamentals-blockchain-architecture
3. Advanced Blockchain Architectures
   https://www.coursera.org/learn/advanced-blockchain-architecture

Use of ICT

Interactive Online Courses

✓ **Advanced Blockchain Architectures on Coursera:** A detailed course covering blockchain architecture, cryptography, node management, and scalability. Perfect for intermediate learners looking to deepen their knowledge.

Research-Based Insights

✓ **Architectural Patterns for Blockchain Systems and Application Design:** A study of 12 architectural patterns derived from 400 real-world blockchain applications. Ideal for understanding design principles and structural aspects of blockchain.

Hands-On Training

✓ **Blockchain Architecture Training by Blockchain Training Alliance:** Instructor-led classes covering blockchain application design, testing, and real-world use cases. Includes certification options.

Applications (Real Life / Industrial)

1. Supply Chain Management

- **Example:** Walmart in China.

  Walmart uses blockchain to track pork suppliers, shippers, and purchasers in China. The distributed ledger ensures transparency, reduces data tampering, and increases efficiency by providing real-time tracking of goods. It improves product traceability, reduces fraud, and enhances supply chain efficiency.

2. Financial Services

- **Example:** UBS Bank

  UBS leverages blockchain-based tokens for cross-border trades, reducing settlement times and costs. It enhances transaction speed, lowers operational costs, and increases transparency in financial settlements.

3. Healthcare

- **Example:** Gem OS

  Gem provides a blockchain operating system that connects siloed healthcare data into a unified platform. This improves patient data management and reduces administrative inefficiencies. It ensures secure patient data sharing, reduces errors, and enhances healthcare delivery.

4. Smart Contracts

- **Example:** Ethereum Blockchain

  Ethereum enables smart contracts that automate agreements between parties without intermediaries. For instance, insurance companies use it to automate claim settlements when predefined conditions are met. It reduces manual intervention, ensures transparency, and minimizes disputes.

5. Digital Identity Management

- **Example:** Factom

  Factom uses blockchain to protect critical government and commercial systems from data theft while ensuring transparency and integrity. It strengthens cybersecurity, prevents identity fraud, and simplifies identity verification processes.

Case-Study (Environmental/Sustainability / Social/Ethical Issues)

A notable case study in blockchain's application to sustainability is the use of blockchain and IoT by platforms like Veridium for carbon credit management. Veridium employs blockchain technology to create a transparent and traceable system for carbon credit trading, addressing issues of fraud and inefficiency in the carbon market. By integrating IoT devices, real-time data on emissions is collected, reducing reliance on self-reported data and enhancing accuracy. Blockchain's immutable ledger ensures that all transactions, including issuance, transfer, and retirement of credits, are recorded transparently, eliminating risks like double counting. This system not only increases accountability but also automates processes through smart contracts, reducing administrative costs and improving market efficiency. Such innovations demonstrate how blockchain can transform carbon markets by fostering trust, transparency, and scalability.

Create Inquisitiveness and Curiosity

Imagine a world where trust is no longer a fragile concept but an unbreakable foundation of every transaction, interaction, and agreement. Blockchain architecture, with its decentralized and immutable design, is revolutionizing how we perceive data security and transparency. At its core, blockchain operates like a digital ledger spread across a peer-to-peer network, where every participant holds a copy of the entire history of transactions. This ingenious system eliminates the need for intermediaries, making processes faster, more secure, and transparent. Picture a supply chain where every product's journey—from raw materials to the final consumer—is permanently recorded and verifiable, ensuring ethical sourcing and sustainability. Or envision a voting system where tampering is impossible, restoring faith in democratic processes. The layered architecture of blockchain—spanning data storage, consensus mechanisms, and user-facing applications—makes it adaptable to countless industries, from finance to healthcare. Yet, its true intrigue lies in its potential to reshape societal norms by fostering decentralized collaboration and trust in ways never seen before. Are you ready to explore how this transformative technology could redefine the future?

Solved Problems (With Increasing Difficulty Level)

1. Problem: Understanding Blockchain Basics (Beginner Level)

Many beginners struggle to understand how blockchain works, including its structure, hashing, and transaction validation.

- **Solution:** A simple JavaScript implementation can help learners grasp the concept. For example, creating a basic blockchain with a genesis block, a chain array, and functions for adding blocks and validating the chain can demystify its core principles.

2. Problem: Energy-Intensive Consensus Mechanisms (Intermediate Level)

Proof-of-Work (PoW) systems like Bitcoin consume significant energy, raising environmental concerns.

- **Solution:** Transitioning to energy-efficient consensus mechanisms like Proof-of-Stake (PoS) has addressed this issue. Ethereum's shift to PoS reduced its energy consumption by 99.95%, demonstrating how blockchain networks can become more sustainable without compromising security.

3. Problem: Scalability Bottlenecks in Layer 1 Blockchains (Advanced Level)

Layer 1 blockchains like Bitcoin and Ethereum face scalability issues, processing only 7–30 transactions per second (TPS), leading to high fees and network congestion.

- **Solution:** Layer 2 solutions such as rollups or sidechains have been implemented to offload transactions from the main chain, significantly improving throughput and reducing costs without sacrificing security.

4. Problem: Lack of Interoperability Between Blockchains (Expert Level)

Different blockchain platforms operate in isolation due to varying protocols and standards, hindering seamless communication and collaboration.

- **Solution:** Cross-chain communication protocols and standardized data formats have been developed to enable interoperability. For instance, Polkadot and Cosmos use relay chains and hubs to connect disparate blockchains, fostering collaboration across ecosystems.

5. Problem: Complexity of Blockchain Adoption in Enterprises (Professional Level)

Enterprises face challenges in integrating blockchain due to its technical complexity, lack of skilled professionals, and regulatory uncertainty.

- **Solution:** Simplified onboarding processes, user-friendly interfaces, and educational initiatives have been introduced to bridge the knowledge gap. Additionally, collaborations between academia, industry experts, and governments are helping create standardized frameworks for smoother adoption.

1.4 BASIC CRYPTO PRIMITIVES

1.4.1 Hash Functions

Hash functions are fundamental cryptographic tools used extensively within blockchain networks. A hash function takes an input (or message) and produces a fixed-length string called a hash value. Hash values serve multiple purposes.

- ✓ Ensuring data integrity by detecting any alterations made post-recording.
- ✓ Linking blocks together through previous block hashes—creating an immutable chain structure.
- ✓ Enabling efficient indexing/searching operations across large datasets stored on ledgers.

Commonly used hash functions include SHA-256 (used by Bitcoin) which generates 256-bit hashes ensuring strong security properties against collisions (two different inputs producing identical outputs).

1.4.2 Digital Signatures

Digital signatures authenticate messages/transactions using asymmetric cryptography.

- ✓ Each user possesses a pair consisting of public/private keys.
- ✓ The private key signs messages creating unique signatures verifiable via corresponding public keys.
- ✓ This ensures authenticity since only legitimate owners possess private keys required for signing actions.

Digital signatures enhance trust among participants by providing non-repudiation allowing senders/receivers certainty regarding origins/validity throughout interactions occurring over networks efficiently.

1.4.3 Encryption Techniques

Encryption techniques safeguard sensitive information stored/transmitted across blockchains.

- ✓ Symmetric encryption uses identical keys for both encryption/decryption processes offering speed but requiring secure key management practices.
- ✓ Asymmetric encryption employs distinct public/private key pairs enhancing security; however; it may introduce latency due increased computational overhead involved during operations performed regularly across networks frequently.

Video Resources
https://www.khanacademy.org/economics-finance-domain/core-finance/money-and-banking/bitcoin/v/bitcoin-cryptographic-hash-function

Use of ICT

https://emn178.github.io/online-tools/sha256.html

Applications (Real Life/Industrial)

One of the most significant applications of hash functions is in **blockchain technology**, where they play a fundamental role in ensuring data integrity, security, and immutability.

In a blockchain, every block contains a unique hash generated by running its data through a cryptographic hash function like SHA-256. This hash acts as a digital fingerprint for the block's contents. Additionally, each block stores the hash of the previous block, creating a linked chain of blocks. If any data in a block is altered, its hash changes entirely due to the "avalanche effect," breaking the chain and making tampering evident. This mechanism ensures that blockchain data remains immutable and secure against unauthorized modifications. Furthermore, hash functions are central to blockchain consensus mechanisms like Proof-of-Work (PoW), where miners solve computational puzzles involving hashes to validate transactions and add new blocks to the chain. This process secures the network while maintaining transparency and trust among participants.

Case-Study (Environmental/Sustainability/Social/Ethical Issues)

Bitcoin mining, particularly through the energy-intensive **Proof-of-Work (PoW)** mechanism, has raised significant environmental and social concerns globally. PoW requires miners to solve complex computational puzzles, which demands substantial electricity and specialized hardware. This process has led to a massive carbon footprint, water usage, and land degradation. For example, a United Nations study revealed that Bitcoin mining during 2020–2021 emitted over **85.89 million tons of CO2**, equivalent to the emissions of Singapore, with 67% of its electricity derived from fossil fuels like coal. In the U.S., the Environmental Working Group (EWG) highlighted how Bitcoin mining operations have revived coal-fired plants in states like Pennsylvania, creating hazardous emissions and harming air quality. Additionally, natural gas plants in New York have been linked to water contamination and overheating aquatic ecosystems.

Socially, communities near mining facilities face challenges such as noise pollution from 24/7 running mining rigs and reduced quality of life. In Georgia and North Carolina, residents report constant low-frequency noise disrupting their daily lives. Furthermore, in Montana and Kentucky, air pollution from mining facilities has been linked to increased health risks for nearby populations. These impacts have sparked global calls for reform in cryptocurrency mining practices. For instance, Ethereum's transition from PoW to the energy-efficient **Proof-of-Stake (PoS)** reduced its energy consumption by 99%, setting an example for Bitcoin to follow. Advocacy campaigns like "Change the Code, Not the Climate" aim to encourage Bitcoin developers and investors to adopt sustainable alternatives.

This case study underscores the urgent need for regulatory interventions and technological innovations to mitigate the environmental and social harms of Bitcoin mining while preserving its economic benefits. Balancing sustainability with technological advancement remains a critical challenge for the cryptocurrency industry.

Create Inquisitiveness and Curiosity

Imagine a world where trust no longer relies on intermediaries but is mathematically guaranteed. How do cryptocurrencies like Bitcoin ensure that transactions are secure, tamper-proof, and authenticated without a central authority? The answer lies in **crypto primitives** like **digital signatures** and **hash functions**, the unsung heroes of blockchain technology. A digital signature acts as a virtual seal, proving ownership and authenticity of a transaction, while hash functions create unique digital fingerprints for data, ensuring integrity and immutability. For instance, when you send Bitcoin, your private key generates a digital signature that only your public key can verify—ensuring the transaction is undeniably yours. Similarly, hash functions link blocks in a blockchain, making any tampering detectable. But here's the twist: what happens if quantum computing threatens these cryptographic systems? Or how are these primitives being used beyond cryptocurrencies, like in securing supply chains or digital identities? Dive deeper into the fascinating world of cryptographic primitives to uncover how they silently power the backbone of decentralized systems and shape the future of secure communication.

Solved Problems (With Increasing Difficulty Level)

1. Problem: Hash Function Verification (Beginner Level)

A file generates a SHA-256 hash value of 5d41402abc4b2a76b9719d911017c592. Verify if the hash matches the original file after downloading.

Solution:

- Compute the SHA-256 hash of the downloaded file using any hashing tool or library.
- Compare the computed hash with 5d41402abc4b2a76b9719d911017c592.
- If they match, the file is intact; otherwise, it has been altered.

2. Problem: Digital Signature Creation (Intermediate Level)

Using the Digital Signature Algorithm (DSA), calculate the signature components r and s for a message m with the following parameters:

- p=23, q=11, g=3, private key x=6, random integer k=7, and hash value H(m)=5.

Solution:

1. Compute $r=(g^{k} \bmod p) \bmod q$

   $r=(3^{7} \bmod 23) \bmod 11=(2187 \bmod 23) \bmod 11=6.$
2. Compute $s=(k^{-1}*(H(m)+x*r)) \bmod q$

- Find $k^{-1} \bmod q$ using modular inverse: $k^{-1}=8$ (since $7*8 \bmod 11=1$).
- Calculate $s=(8*(5+6*6)) \bmod 11=(8*(5+36)) \bmod 11=(8*41) \bmod 11=328 \bmod 11=9$

Thus, the signature is (r,s)=(6,9)(r, s) = (6, 9)(r,s)=(6,9).

1.5 HASHCHAIN TO BLOCKCHAIN

The concept of hashchains serves as an initial step towards understanding blockchain structures.

- ✓ A hashchain consists merely linking hashes sequentially where each hash references itspredecessor forming linear chains. However; blockchains take this concept further.
- ✓ Blocks contain multiple transactions bundled together along with metadata including timestamps & nonce values required during mining processes. - Each block references previous blocks' hashes ensuring immutability & continuity throughout entire chains effectively.

This design enables efficient validation processes since miners only need verify last few blocks rather than entire history when confirming new additions made periodically over time resulting improved scalability overall.

Video Resources
https://www.youtube.com/watch?v=iYYf3w4RPDA

Use of ICT

https://andersbrownworth.com/blockchain/

Applications (Real Life / Industrial)

Blockchain technology, built upon the principles of hashchains, has revolutionized electronic voting by addressing key challenges such as security, transparency, and voter trust. Traditional voting systems often face issues like tampering, unauthorized access, and lack of verifiability. Blockchain overcomes these problems by creating an immutable and decentralized ledger where each vote is recorded as a transaction linked to a cryptographic hash. This ensures that votes cannot be altered or deleted once cast. Additionally, blockchain enables real-time auditability, where voters can verify that their vote has been recorded accurately without compromising anonymity. For example, blockchain-based voting systems allow overseas voters to securely cast their ballots via mobile devices, reducing logistical barriers and increasing participation. Governments and organizations worldwide are exploring blockchain for elections to ensure tamper-proof records and transparent results, fostering trust in democratic processes.

Case-Study (Environmental/Sustainability/Social/Ethical Issues)

The evolution from hashchain to blockchain has brought significant advancements in transparency, security, and decentralization, but it also raises critical environmental and sustainability concerns. Blockchain networks, particularly those using energy-intensive **Proof-of-Work (PoW)** consensus mechanisms, have been criticized for their substantial carbon footprint. For example, Bitcoin's PoW mining process consumes vast amounts of electricity, with its carbon emissions in 2019 equaling that of Switzerland. This energy demand stems from the computational power required to solve cryptographic puzzles and secure the network.

To address these issues, alternative consensus mechanisms like **Proof-of-Stake (PoS)** have emerged as more sustainable options. Ethereum's transition to PoS in 2022 reduced its energy consumption by over 99%, demonstrating the potential for blockchain technology to align with environmental goals. Beyond energy efficiency, blockchain is being leveraged for sustainability initiatives such as carbon credit tracking, renewable energy trading, and waste management. For instance, platforms like Power Ledger enable peer-to-peer energy trading, allowing homeowners to sell excess solar power directly to others

However, challenges remain. The scalability of blockchain systems and the accuracy of data input are critical for ensuring meaningful environmental impact. Additionally, widespread adoption of sustainable blockchain practices requires global collaboration and regulatory frameworks. Despite these hurdles, blockchain's ability to enhance transparency and accountability makes it a promising tool for addressing climate change and promoting sustainable development across industries.

Create Inquisitiveness And Curiosity

Have you ever wondered how blockchain technology guarantees trust in a world without intermediaries? At its core lies the fascinating concept of **hashchains**, the precursor to modern blockchains. A hashchain is like a digital fingerprint trail—each piece of data is transformed into a unique hash, and these hashes are linked together in a sequence. But here's where it gets exciting: blockchain takes this idea further by creating a decentralized, tamper-proof ledger where each block contains not only its own data but also the hash of the previous block. This ingenious design ensures that even the slightest alteration in one block disrupts the entire chain, making fraud virtually impossible.

Now think about this. How does this technology power cryptocurrencies, secure supply chains, and even enable transparent voting systems? Why is it that blockchain can prevent double-spending in digital currencies or ensure the authenticity of your food's origin? And with advancements like Ethereum's smart contracts, how has blockchain evolved beyond its hashchain roots to reshape industries like healthcare and finance? Dive deeper into this transformative journey from hashchain to blockchain to uncover how it's revolutionizing trust, transparency, and security in our digital world.

Solved Problems (With Increasing Difficulty Level)

Consider a simple hashchain where each block contains a unique transaction and a hash of the previous block. Suppose we have three blocks: Block A, Block B, and Block C. The hash of Block A is `H(A) = 1234`, the hash of Block B is `H(B) = 5678`, and the hash of Block C is `H(C) = 9012`. Each block also includes the hash of the previous block. Block A does not have a previous block, so it only contains its own hash. Block B contains `H(A)` and its own hash, and Block C contains `H(B)` and its own hash.

Challenge

If Block B's transaction data is altered, how does this affect the hashchain, and what mathematical properties of hash functions are involved in detecting this change?

Solution

1. **Initial Setup:**
    - **Block A:** `{Transaction A, H(A) = 1234}`
    - **Block B:** `{Transaction B, H(A) = 1234, H(B) = 5678}`
    - **Block C:** `{Transaction C, H(B) = 5678, H(C) = 9012}`
2. **Altering Block B:**
    - Suppose the transaction data in Block B is altered. This changes its hash from `5678` to a new value, say `1111`.
3. **Impact on Hashchain:**
    - The new Block B becomes `{Altered Transaction B, H(A) = 1234, New H(B) = 1111}`.
    - Block C, which contains `H(B) = 5678`, no longer matches the new hash of Block B (`1111`). This breaks the hashchain.
4. **Mathematical Properties Involved:**
    - **Determinism:** Hash functions always produce the same output for a given input. Therefore, altering Block B's data changes its hash predictably.
    - **Collision Resistance:** It is computationally infeasible to find two different inputs with the same hash output. This ensures that altering Block B's data will not accidentally produce the same hash as before.

- **Avalanche Effect:** A small change in the input results in a significant change in the output hash. This property makes it easy to detect alterations by comparing hashes.

By leveraging these properties, blockchain technology ensures that any tampering with the data in a block is detectable, maintaining the integrity and security of the hashchain-turned-blockchain.

1.6 BASIC CONSENSUS MECHANISMS

Consensus mechanisms play pivotal roles ensuring agreement among distributed nodes regarding state updates occurring within ledgers.

Proof-of-Work (PoW)

PoW requires miners compete solving complex mathematical puzzles validating transactions before adding new blocks onto chains.While secure & decentralized; it consumes significant computational resources leading environmental concerns raised frequently nowadays prompting exploration alternative methods gaining popularity recently.

Proof-of-Stake (PoS)

PoS allows validators create new blocks based upon ownership stakes held rather than computational power expended.This method promotes energy efficiency reducing carbon footprints associated mining activities prevalent within traditional PoW models significantly improving sustainability efforts overall.

Delegated Proof-of-Stake (DPoS)

In DPoS systems stakeholders elect representatives validating transactions on behalf others enhancing scalability while maintaining decentralization principles intact effectively.

Practical Byzantine Fault Tolerance (PBFT)

PBFT addresses challenges posed malicious actors attempting disrupt consensus processes within permissioned networks ensuring reliability critical applications requiring high levels trustworthiness amongst participants involved consistently throughout interactions occurring regularly.

Understanding blockchain architecture alongside its design principlesincluding cryptographic primitives such as hash functions/digital signatures/encryption techniquesprovides insights into how these technologies operate effectively addressing challenges present within existing systems today. By leveraging diverse consensus mechanisms tailored towards specific requirements developers can create robust solutions meeting user needs efficiently moving forward into future challenges ahead.

Video Resources
https://www.youtube.com/watch?v=NqgzF63yNcU&t=2s

Use of ICT

https://kriptomat.io/learn/academy/blockchain-fundamentals/blockchain-consensus-mechanisms/

Applications (Real Life / Industrial)

In Internet of Things, Consensus mechanisms secure communication and data exchange between IoT devices. This enhances the reliability and security of smart home and industrial IoT applications.

Case-Study (Environmental/Sustainability/Social/Ethical Issues)

Consensus mechanisms in blockchain technology also raise important social and ethical considerations. One significant issue is the **centralization of power** in some consensus algorithms. For instance, **Proof-of-Stake (PoS)** systems can concentrate control among large stakeholders, as validators with more "staked" cryptocurrency have a higher chance of being selected to create new blocks. This can lead to a situation where a small group of validators dominate the network, undermining the decentralized ethos of blockchain. Another ethical concern is **access inequality**.

The high computational requirements of **-of-Work (PoW)** systems mean that only those with access to powerful hardware and cheap electricity can participate in mining, excluding many individuals and communities from contributing to the network. This can exacerbate existing social inequalities by limiting opportunities for participation and economic empowerment.

Furthermore, the use of blockchain in **voting systems** raises ethical questions about privacy and security. While consensus mechanisms can ensure the integrity of votes, they must also protect voter anonymity and prevent coercion. Ensuring that these systems are accessible and secure for all users is a critical ethical challenge.In response to these issues, developers are exploring more inclusive consensus mechanisms, such as **Delegated Proof-of-Stake (DPoS)**, which allows users to vote for validators, promoting greater decentralization and community involvement. Additionally, initiatives focusing on renewable energy and accessible hardware are underway to make blockchain participation more equitable. This case study highlights the need for consensus mechanisms to balance technological innovation with social responsibility and ethical considerations.

Create Inquisitiveness and Curiosity

Imagine a world where thousands of computers, scattered across the globe, work together to agree on a single version of truth—without ever meeting or trusting each other. How is this even possible? Enter **consensus mechanisms**, the invisible force behind blockchain technology. These protocols ensure that every transaction is valid, secure, and tamper-proof, even in a decentralized system.

But here's where it gets fascinating: Why does Bitcoin rely on energy hungry **Proof-of-Work (PoW)**, while Ethereum has transitioned to the eco-friendly **Proof-of-Stake (PoS)**? What about newer models like **Delegated Proof-of-Stake (DPoS)** or **Byzantine Fault Tolerance (BFT)**—how do they solve problems like scalability and security? And did you know that some consensus mechanisms, like **Proof-of-Authority (PoA)**, sacrifice decentralization for speed and efficiency?

Think about this: Can consensus mechanisms evolve to handle global challenges like sustainability or even power artificial intelligence systems? Dive deeper into this topic to uncover how these algorithms are shaping the future of trustless systems and revolutionizing industries worldwide!

Solved Problems (With Increasing Difficulty Level)

In a blockchain network using the **Proof-of-Work (PoW)** consensus mechanism, miners compete to solve a cryptographic puzzle. The puzzle involves finding a nonce (n) such that the hash of the block data concatenated with nnn produces a hash value with at least **4 leading zeros** in hexadecimal format.

Given the Block Data

- `Block Data = "Transaction123"` and the hash function H(x)=SHA−256(x)

Find the smallest nonce (nnn) such that H("Transaction123"+n)H("Transaction123" + n)H("Transaction123"+n) starts with at least 4 leading zeros.

Solution

1. **Understand the Problem:**
   - The goal is to find a nonce (nnn) such that when it is appended to the block data and hashed, the resulting hash begins with "0000".
   - Hashing is deterministic, so we can brute-force by incrementing nnn until the condition is satisfied.
2. **Algorithm:**
   - Start with n=0
   - Concatenate the block data with n: `data_with_nonce = "Transaction123" + str(n).`
   - Compute H(datawithnonce)using SHA-256.
   - Check if the resulting hash starts with "0000". If not, increment nnn and repeat.
3. **Implementation (Python Code):**

```
python
import hashlib
block_data ="Transaction123"
nonce =0
whileTrue:
# Concatenate block data with nonce
data_with_nonce = block_data +str(nonce)
# Compute SHA-256 hash
hash_result =hashlib.sha256(data_with_nonce.encode()).hexdigest()
# Check if hash starts with 4 leading zeros
if hash_result[:4]=="0000":
print(f"Nonce found: {nonce}")
print(f"Hash: {hash_result}")
break
# Increment nonce
nonce +=1
```

4. Explanation of Output:

- The code will output the smallest nonce (nnn) that satisfies the condition.
- **For example, if the result is:**

  text

  Nonce found: 1048576

  Hash: 0000a3f2d9e8b7c6...

  This means that appending 1048576 to "Transaction123" produces a valid hash starting with "0000".

5. **Key Concepts Demonstrated:**

- **Determinism of Hash Functions:** The same input always producesthe same output.
- **Brute Force in PoW:** Miners must try multiple nonces until they find one that satisfies the difficulty level.
- **Difficulty Adjustment:** Increasing or decreasing the number of required leading zeros adjusts how hard it is to find a valid nonce.

This problem illustrates how PoW ensures consensus by requiring computational effort to validate blocks, making tampering infeasible due to the high cost of recomputing hashes for altered blocks.

SUMMARY

- **Introduction to Blockchain Evolution**: Covers the transition from digital money to distributed ledgers.
- **Blockchain Design Primitives**: Explains key components such as protocols, security, consensus mechanisms, permissions, and privacy.
- **Blockchain Architecture**: Discusses the structure and components of blockchain systems.
- **Cryptographic Fundamentals**: Introduces hashing and digital signatures as essential cryptographic tools.
- **Consensus Mechanisms**: Explains basic methods for achieving agreement in decentralized networks.

EXERCISES

A. Subjective Questions

Category-I *(Revised Bloom's Level 1, 2 & 3)*

1. Remembering (Level 1)

- Define the key components of blockchain architecture and explain the role of basic cryptographic primitives such as hash functions and digital signatures in ensuring data integrity and security.

2. Understanding (Level 2)

- Describe how consensus mechanisms like Proof-of-Work (PoW) and Proof-of-Stake (PoS) operate. Compare their effectiveness in maintaining trust and decentralization in distributed ledger systems.

3. Applying (Level 3)

- Given a scenario where a blockchain system is being designed for a healthcare application, explain how the transition from hashchain to blockchain and the choice of consensus mechanism can address privacy, security, and scalability concerns.

Category-II *(Revised Bloom's Level-4, 5 & 6)*

1. Analyzing (Level 4)

- Analyze the relationship between blockchain architecture design and the choice of consensus mechanisms. How does the selection of a specific consensus mechanism (e.g., Proof-of-Work, Proof-of-Stake) impact the scalability, security, and energy efficiency of a blockchain system?

2. Evaluating (Level 5)

- Evaluate the effectiveness of cryptographic primitives like hash functions and digital signatures in addressing privacy and security concerns in distributed ledger systems. Discuss their limitations in practical applications such as financial transactions or healthcare data management.

3. Creating (Level 6)

- Design a blockchain-based solution for a supply chain management system. Specify how you would integrate cryptographic primitives, hashchain-to-blockchain transition, and a suitable consensus mechanism to ensure transparency, security, and scalability. Justify your design choices.

B. Objective Questions

Category-I *(Revised Bloom's Level-1, 2 & 3)*

1. Remembering (Level 1)

- What is the primary purpose of a hash function in blockchain technology?
  - (a) To encrypt data for secure communication
  - (b) To link blocks together and ensure data integrity
  - (c) To store transaction details in a database
  - (d) To manage permissions in a blockchain network

2. Understanding (Level 2)

- How does a consensus mechanism contribute to the functionality of a distributed ledger?
  - (a) By ensuring that all nodes agree on the validity of transactions
  - (b) By encrypting data to maintain privacy
  - (c) By allowing only authorized users to access the ledger
  - (d) By storing transaction data in a centralized database

3. Applying (Level 3)

- A blockchain network uses Proof-of-Work (PoW) as its consensus mechanism. If a malicious actor attempts to alter the data in one block, what will happen to the rest of the chain?

(a) The altered block will be automatically removed from the chain.
(b) The hash values of all subsequent blocks will change, making tampering vident.
(c) The network will accept the changes as long as they are minor.
(d) The altered block will remain unchanged, but future blocks will be unaffected.

Category-II (Revised Bloom's Level-4, 5 & 6)

1. Analyzing (Level 4)

- Which of the following factors is most critical when analyzing the impact of consensus mechanisms on blockchain scalability?

(a) Energy consumption
(b) Network latency
(c) Block size
(d) All of the above

2. Evaluating (Level 5)

- Evaluate the following statement: "Proof-of-Stake (PoS) consensus mechanisms are more energy-efficient than Proof-of-Work (PoW) mechanisms." Which of the following best describes the implications of this statement?

(a) PoS reduces energy consumption but increases centralization.
(b) PoS increases energy consumption but reduces centralization.
(c) PoS has no impact on energy consumption or centralization.
(d) PoS reduces energy consumption and maintains decentralization.

3. Creating (Level 6)

- When designing a blockchain-based supply chain system, which of the following consensus mechanisms would be most appropriate for ensuring both security and scalability?

(a) Proof-of-Work (PoW)
(b) Proof-of-Stake (PoS)
(c) Delegated Proof-of-Stake (DPoS)
(d) Byzantine Fault Tolerance (BFT)

TEACHER'S KNOW MORE

- **Advanced Cryptographic Techniques:**
  - **Homomorphic Encryption:** Allows computations to be performed directly on encrypted data.
  - **Zero-Knowledge Proofs:** Enables verification of transactions without revealing underlying data.
- **Blockchain Scalability Solutions:**
  - **Sharding:** Divides the network into smaller groups to process transactions in parallel.
  - **Off-Chain Transactions:** Processes transactions outside the main blockchain to reduce congestion.
- **Blockchain Governance Models:**
  - **Decentralized Governance:** Empowers users to participate in decision-making processes.
  - **Centralized Governance:** Involves a central authority controlling updates and changes.

- **Blockchain Interoperability**:
  - **Cross-Chain Bridges**: Enables the transfer of assets between different blockchain networks.
- **Blockchain Security Threats**:
  - **51% Attack**: A scenario where a group controls more than half of the network's mining power.
  - **Smart Contract Vulnerabilities**: Errors in smart contract code can lead to financial losses or security breaches.

UNIT 2

Consensus

RATIONALE

Consensus protocols are essential in distributed systems, particularly in blockchain technology, where they ensure that all nodes agree on a common value or sequence of values despite potential failures or malicious behavior. This unit explores the requirements, mechanisms, and benefits of various consensus protocols, with a focus on Proof of Work (PoW), and considers their impact on blockchain design.

OUTCOMES

- Understand the key requirements for consensus protocols.
- Explain the Proof of Work (PoW) consensus mechanism, its purpose, innovation, and benefits.
- Discuss the scalability aspects of blockchain consensus protocols.
- Describe the design goals and consensus protocols suitable for permissioned blockchains.

2.1 REQUIREMENTS FOR CONSENSUS PROTOCOLS

The need for consensus protocols originated from challenges like the Byzantine Generals Problem in distributed computing. Effective consensus protocols generally include several key properties. These properties ensure that distributed systems can function reliably and securely, even when faced with challenges such as network failures, malicious actors, or inconsistent data.

- **Agreement:** All correct (i.e., non-faulty) processes must agree on the same value. This is the foundational requirement for any consensus protocol. Without agreement, the system cannot maintain a consistent state, leading to conflicts and unreliable operations. Reaching agreement ensures that every participant in the network comes to a uniform decision, which is crucial for maintaining consistency across the system.
- **Termination:** Every correct process must eventually decide on some value. This property guarantees that the protocol will not run indefinitely and that all non-faulty nodes will reach a conclusion within a reasonable timeframe. Without termination, a system could stall indefinitely, preventing it from processing new information or responding to changing conditions.
- **Integrity (or Validity):** Integrity ensures that the decisions made by the consensus protocol are valid and trustworthy.

- ✓ **Weak Validity:** For each correct process, its output must be the input of some correct process. This means that if a process proposes a value, it should be reflected in the final consensus if it is to be considered valid. If a process proposes a certain data value, the final consensus should reflect the input of at least one correct process.
- ✓ **Strong Validity:** If all correct processes propose the same input value, they must all output that value. This ensures that consensus reflects the actual inputs when there is unanimous agreement among correct nodes. This is a stronger guarantee than weak validity.
- ✓ **Fault Tolerance:** Consensus protocols must be resilient to a certain number of faulty or malicious processes. Fault tolerance is crucial for ensuring that the system can continue to operate correctly even when some nodes fail or attempt to disrupt the process. For instance, a protocol is termed t-resilient if it can achieve consensus even when up to t processes fail. This implies the protocol should be able to tolerate and mitigate failures from a portion of its nodes.

2.1.1 Performance Metrics

- **Latency:** The time taken to reach consensus can vary based on network conditions and the number of nodes involved.
- **Throughput:** The number of transactions processed in a given time frame is critical for evaluating efficiency. High throughput ensures that the system can handle a large volume of transactions.
- **Message Complexity:** This refers to the amount of communication required between nodes during the consensus process, impacting overall performance. Reducing message complexity can lead to more efficient and scalable consensus protocols.
- **Security Considerations:** While not always directly part of the consensus requirements, security against attacks and ensuring data integrity are vital as they help maintain trust within the network. Security mechanisms such as cryptographic signatures and secure communication channels are essential for protecting against malicious actors.

2.1.2 Common Consensus Protocols

- **Proof of Work (PoW):** Used by Bitcoin, this method requires computational effort to validate transactions.
- **Proof of Stake (PoS):** In PoS, validators are chosen based on their stake in the network rather than computational power.
- **Practical Byzantine Fault Tolerance (PBFT):** This protocol is designed to work effectively even in environments where some nodes may act maliciously or fail.

These requirements and properties are crucial for designing robust consensus protocols that ensure reliability and integrity in distributed systems, particularly as they scale and face various operational challenges. Understanding these foundational elements is key to appreciating the design and trade-offs involved in different consensus mechanisms.

Video Resources
https://www.youtube.com/watch?v=9B8Z8gN3QkA

Use of ICT

A simplified version of a distributed system simulator like "SimBlock" or a custom-built interactive web application using JavaScript and a visualization library like D3.js. This interactive simulation would provide a hands-on learning experience, allowing students to directly observe the impact of different factors on the ability of a distributed system to achieve consensus. This will reinforce their understanding of the key requirements for consensus protocols, such as agreement, termination, integrity, and fault tolerance, in a more engaging and memorable way.

Applications

Distributed databases, cloud computing, and blockchain technology.

Case Study

Proof of work is a core mechanism that facilitates Bitcoin transactions by enabling the network to agree on the order of transactions and blocks, ensuring that all nodes agree with one another; in a proof-of-work system, the first node to solve a given problem receives a reward for its effort, using computer resources like electricity and storage to mine cryptocurrency. Proposed by Markus Jakobsson and Ari Juels in 1999, the innovation of Proof of Work provides a decentralized way to verify transactions without a centralized database, later refined in the Bitcoin network as block mining, requiring miners to solve an expensive mathematical puzzle to add transactions to the blockchain and earn rewards. The purpose of POW is to achieve consensus in a distributed system by forcing miners to compete to solve a complicated math problem with high levels of randomness, preventing any single party from blocking other nodes from reaching consensus. The mechanism behind Proof of Work involves solving complex mathematical problems, and it benefits the blockchain by providing no single point of failure, enhancing security and privacy, allowing instantaneous transactions, being energy-efficient, and being cost-effective, as miners are incentivized to expend more computing power, making the network more secure for users.

Create Inquisitiveness And Curiosity

What are the theoretical limits on achieving consensus in asynchronous networks with potentially malicious actors? How do different consensus protocols approach these limits?

Solved Problems

Problem: Assume a simplified consensus protocol where nodes exchange messages and require a simple majority to agree on a value. If there are 7 nodes, how many faulty nodes can the system tolerate while still achieving consensus?

Solution: The system requires a simple majority to agree. Therefore, more than half the nodes must be correct. With 7 nodes, a majority is 4 (since 3 nodes is less than half and 4 are more than half). Thus, to have a majority to agree on a value, there must be 4 non-faulty nodes to come to an agreement. To do this, the system is tolerant to 3 nodes. Therefore, the system is 3-resilient.

2.2 PROOF OF WORK (POW)

Proof of Work (PoW) was initially conceived as a method to deter email spamming. **Proof of Work (PoW)** is a core mechanism that facilitates Bitcoin transactions. It's a consensus algorithm that enables the network to agree on the order of transactions and blocks. In other words, it's a way to ensure that all nodes (computers on the network) agree with one another about which transactions are valid and in what order they occurred.In a proof-of-work system, the first node to solve a given problem receives a reward for its effort. This means that if you have a computer with access to computational resources, like electricity and processing power, you can use that resource to mine cryptocurrency.

Proof of work is a concept in computer science and cryptography whereby a piece of data must be difficult (or computationally expensive) to produce without the consent of the person or entity using the data. The proof of work prevents users from creating alternative chains and thus gaining control over the system. The blockchain incorporates a public ledger that records transactions on a digital ledger, but unlike a traditional database, it uses cryptography to ensure data integrity and prevents tampering with information.

Proof of work is a consensus algorithm that allows the network to agree on the validity of transactions. For a transaction in the blockchain, it must be validated by the network. This can be done using several different ways. Proof of Work (PoW) is the first and most popular method. In this method, miners compete with each other to solve complex mathematical problems to validate transactions. If a miner solves these problems quickly enough, they will be rewarded with newly created Bitcoins and added to the blockchain.

2.2.1 Innovation of Proof of Work

The innovation of Proof of Work, proposed by Markus Jakobsson and Ari Juels in 1999, has been one of the most critical developments in cryptocurrency. It is a new way to verify transactions in a distributed network. The original idea was to create a system that would be implemented on top of existing P2P networks. Markus Jakobsson and Ari Juels, in 1999, used a combination of hashing and proof-of-work to achieve a distributed consensus among nodes about the order of transactions. The scheme was called "Proof-of-Work" (PoW). Their key innovation was linking computational effort to the validation process.

The concept was later refined and implemented on top of the Bitcoin network, where it became known as block mining. The PoW scheme is called Proof-of-Work because Bitcoin miners need to solve a computationally intensive mathematical puzzle before adding the transaction to the blockchain and earning themselves a reward. The puzzle is designed to take a large amount of computational power to solve, making it hard for a single entity to control the network's mining process. This prevents one entity from gaining a majority over the hashing power and censoring transactions. This system is also designed so that blocks cannot be added until they are signed by many users, preventing one entity from gaining too much control over the system. The original idea behind the proof-of-work scheme was to provide a way for miners to avoid centralization. The proof-of-work scheme is designed such that any miner can generate a block, but only the first miner to solve the problem gets a reward. This system creates a computational requirement for new blocks, called the proof of work, or PoW.

2.2.2 Purpose of Proof of Work (PoW)

The purpose of proof of work (PoW) is to achieve consensus in a distributed system. Consensus is the state where all participants agree on a single value. In a system with POW, if one party does not agree with the majority, it will not be able to reach a consensus and, therefore, cannot reach a consensus on the value being verified. This prevents the problem of one person having a majority hash, which would allow them to block other nodes from reaching consensus.

The miner who solves a block first gets to add it to the blockchain and get paid some reward for doing so, but if multiple miners are trying to solve blocks at the same time, then one of them will win and be able to create another block on top of theirs (and claim their reward). This problem can be solved by forcing all miners to compete with each other for each new block created, which requires solving a complicated math problem with high levels of randomness involved.All nodes on the network must validate the block before it is added to the chain; this ensures no one person controls more than 51% of hashing power on any given network and that no group or entity has centralized control over the network or can manipulate it for their benefit (note: Bitcoin uses Proof-of-Work insteadof Proof of Stake).

2.2.3 Mechanism of Proof of Work

The mechanism of Proof of Work (PoW) as given in figure 2.1 is an essential topic in the world of cryptocurrencies. The concept of PoW is that a computer has to expend work to validate a block. This validation process is performed by solving a problem requiring computers to solve math problems.

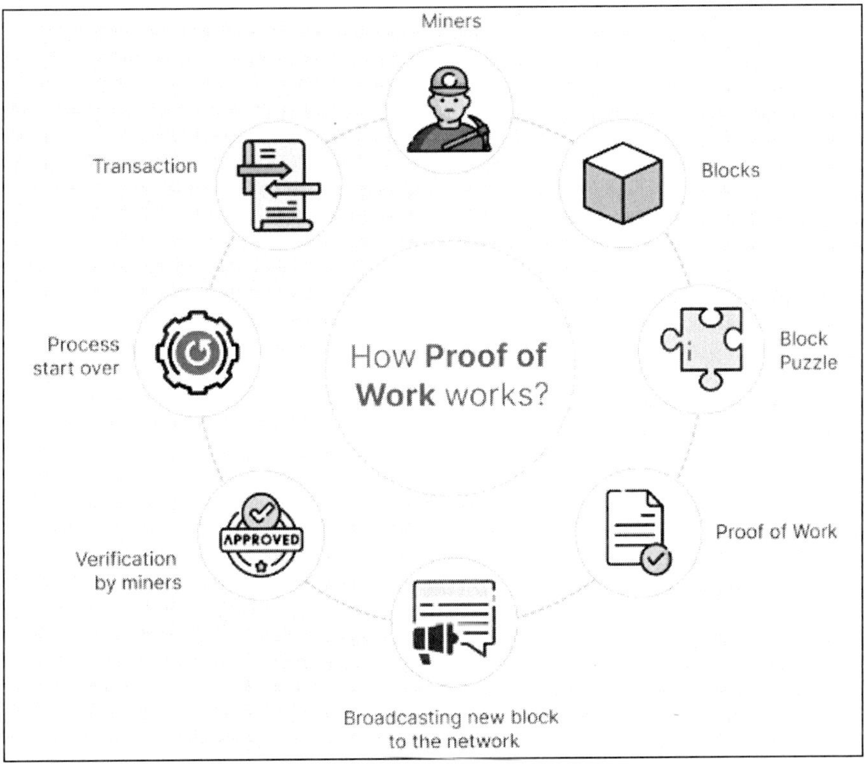

Figure 2.1: *Mechanism of Proof of Work*

The problem is called the hash function, which takes user input and outputs many numbers. Other computers on the network verify the output. This verification process is known as mining, and it takes place when users choose to mine for cryptocurrency or participate in the network.

With PoW, miners solve complex mathematical problems called 'blocks' to add them to the blockchain. When they solve these blocks, they are rewarded with new bitcoins. This is done through POW mining. Proof of Work (PoW) is a distributed consensus algorithm that makes it difficult to fake or reverse engineer the history of a transaction. It also makes it expensive to attack the network.Proof of work is a consensus algorithm used in cryptocurrencies to verify the legitimacy of an arbitrary number of transactions. It works by having a vast network of participants (miners) do work to find an appropriate number (hence "proof") for a block of transactions called a nonce. The miner who solves the proof receives a reward in the form of cryptocurrency. The primary purpose of proof of work is to ensure that no one can cheat the system by making any extra blocks. This prevents double spending by allowing only one piece of data per block. The secondary purpose is also to ensure that anyone attempting to hack the system cannot simply rewrite all past blocks as new ones since they would not receive any reward for doing so.

2.2.4 Benefits of Proof of Work (PoW)

Proof of Work(POW) is a consensus algorithm requiring participants to solve a computationally-intensive problem before they are allowed to participate in the network. This ensures that only participants with real computational power can participate and make decisions.The benefits of Proof of Work (PoW) include the following as given in figure 2.2.

***Figure 2.2:** Benefits of Proof of Work*

- **No Single Point of Failure:** The system cannot be hacked or attacked by any individual, group, or entity.
- **Secure:** It offers complete security and privacy protection to users from various threats such as hacking, theft, or data loss.
- **Instantaneous Transactions:** POW allows instant transactions between parties without requiring third parties like banks or governments to facilitate such transactions.

- **Energy Efficient** Blockchains are energy efficient because they use a proof-of-work (POW) mechanism to validate transactions.
- **Cost Effective**In PoW, miners compete with each other to solve complicated mathematical problems. The first miner to solve it gets rewarded with the block reward and transaction fees from the new block. This incentivizes miners to expend more computing power on the network, making it more secure for users.

Video Resources
https://www.youtube.com/watch?v=9rHbB1ph3Fk

Use of ICT

https://www.coursera.org/specializations/blockchain

Applications

Bitcoin, Litecoin, and other cryptocurrencies.

Case Study

A notable case study for Proof of Work is Bitcoin, the first widely adopted cryptocurrency to utilize this consensus mechanism. Bitcoin's implementation of PoW requires miners to solve complex cryptographic puzzles, which demands significant computational effort and energy consumption. This process ensures the security and integrity of the blockchain by making it computationally impractical for any single entity to alter transaction history.

For instance, Bitcoin's network adjusts its difficulty target every 2016 blocks to maintain a consistent block creation time, typically around 10 minutes. This mechanism has proven effective in maintaining network security and decentralization, as seen in Bitcoin's resilience against major attacks.

However, the high energy consumption has led to discussions about sustainability and scalability, prompting exploration of alternative consensus mechanisms like Proof of Stake. Despite these challenges, Bitcoin remains a robust example of how Proof of Work can secure a decentralized network without a central authority.

Create Inquisitiveness and Curiosity

Given the high energy consumption of PoW, what are the potential long-term impacts on the environment, and what are the alternative solutions?

Solved Problems

A miner has a hash rate of 15 TH/s. The network hash rate is 150 EH/s. What is the miner's probability of finding the next block, assuming a block time of 10 minutes?

Solution

First, convert the hash rates to the same units. 1 EH/s = 10^18 H/s and 1 TH/s = 10^12 H/s. The miner's proportion of the network hash rate is (15 * 10^12) / (150 * 10^18) = 10^-7. The probability of finding the next block is approximately equal to their proportion of the total hash rate. Therefore, the probability is 10^-7 or 0.00001%.

2.3 SCALABILITY ASPECTS OF BLOCKCHAIN CONSENSUS PROTOCOLS

Scalability is a major bottleneck for the widespread adoption of blockchain technology. The scalability of blockchain consensus protocols refers to their ability to handle a growing number of transactions and users without compromising performance, security, or decentralization.

One of the primary challenges in blockchain technology is addressing the trade-off between these three properties, often referred to as the "scalability trilemma." Here's a more detailed look at the scalability aspects:

2.3.1 Limitations of PoW

While Proof of Work (PoW) has proven to be a secure and reliable consensus mechanism, it faces significant limitations in terms of scalability. The computational intensity required for mining and the need for block propagation across the network can lead to low transaction throughput and long confirmation times. This can hinder the ability of PoW-based blockchains to handle a large volume of transactions efficiently.

2.3.2 Alternative Consensus Mechanisms

To overcome the scalability limitations of PoW, researchers and developers have proposed alternative consensus mechanisms, such as

- **Proof of Stake (PoS):** In PoS, validators are chosen based on their stake (i.e., the amount of cryptocurrency they hold) in the network. PoS can offer faster transaction confirmation times and higher throughput compared to PoW, as it eliminates the need for energy-intensive mining.
- **Delegated Proof of Stake (DPoS):** DPoS is a variant of PoS where token holders delegate their voting power to a smaller set of validators, who are then responsible for block creation and transaction validation. DPoS can achieve even higher scalability than PoS by reducing the number of nodes involved in the consensus process.

2.3.3 Layer-2 Scaling Solutions

Layer-2 scaling solutions are techniques that enable transactions to be processed off-chain, reducing the burden on the main blockchain and improving scalability. Some popular layer-2 solutions include

- **Lightning Network:** The Lightning Network is a layer-2 protocol that allows for off-chain transactions with on-chain settlement. It enables participants to create payment channels and conduct multiple transactions within those channels without broadcasting each transaction to the main blockchain.
- **State Channels:** Similar to the Lightning Network, state channels allow for private, off-chain interactions between participants. State channels can be used for a variety of applications, such as payment processing, gaming, and decentralized exchanges.

Video Resources
https://www.youtube.com/watch?v=UyxDaPGIXig

Use of ICT

https://shardeum.org/blog/what-is-blockchain-scalability/

Applications

Blockchain platforms requiring high transaction throughput, such as payment systems and decentralized exchanges.

Case Study

A notable case study on scalability in blockchain consensus protocols is the implementation of **Delegated Proof of Stake (DPoS)** by the EOS blockchain. EOS faced significant scalability challenges with its initial consensus mechanism, which limited its transaction throughput. By adopting DPoS, EOS was able to significantly enhance its scalability, allowing for thousands of transactions per second. This was achieved by reducing the number of validators required to validate transactions, thereby increasing network efficiency and reducing latency. Additionally, EOS utilized a **horizontal scaling** approach by implementing a multi-chain architecture, where transactions are processed across multiple parallel chains, further enhancing scalability. This approach not only improved transaction processing speed but also maintained decentralization and security, making EOS a robust example of how scalable consensus protocols can support high-performance blockchain networks.

Create Inquisitiveness and Curiosity

What are the long-term implications of different scaling solutions on the decentralization and security of blockchain networks?

Solved Problems

A blockchain has a block size of 2 MB and a block time of 15 seconds. If each transaction is 400 bytes on average, what is the theoretical maximum transaction throughput (TPS)?

Solution

2 MB = 2048 KB = 2048 * 1024 bytes.

Number of transactions per block = (2048 * 1024)/400 = 5242.88 (approximately 5242).
Block time = 15 seconds.

TPS = 5242 / 15 = 349.47 TPS (approximately 349).

2.4 PERMISSIONED BLOCKCHAINS: DESIGN GOALS

Permissioned blockchains are often used in enterprise settings to provide increased control and privacy.Permissioned blockchains, as given in figure 2.3 also known as private or consortium blockchains, are blockchain networks where participation is restricted to a select group of authorized participants.

Unlike public blockchains like Bitcoin, permissioned blockchains offer greater control over who can access and validate data, making them suitable for various enterprise and regulated environments. Here's a more detailed look at their design goals and consensus protocols.

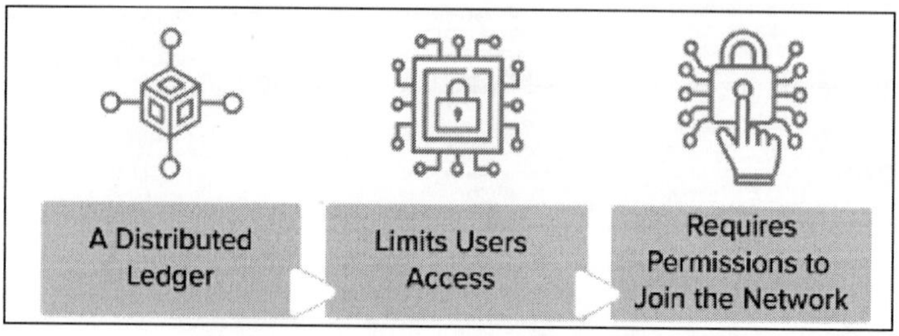

Figure 2.3: *Permissioned Blockchain*

2.4.1 Design Goals of Permissioned Blockchains

- **Access Control:** One of the primary design goals of permissioned blockchains is to control who can participate in the network. This is typically achieved through identity management and access control mechanisms, ensuring that only authorized participants can access and validate data.
- **Privacy:** Permissioned blockchains often prioritize privacy by limiting the visibility of transaction data to authorized participants. This can be achieved through techniques such as data encryption, zero-knowledge proofs, and selective disclosure of information.
- **Regulatory Compliance:** Permissioned blockchains are designed to comply with industry-specific regulations and legal requirements. This may involve implementing features such as data retention policies, audit trails, and reporting mechanisms.

Video Resources
https://www.youtube.com/watch?v=rmNrWS3sjDg

Use of ICT

Information and Communication Technology (ICT) enables the design goals of permissioned blockchains by integrating tools like access control systems (e.g., digital identity verification) to restrict participation to authorized entities, optimized consensus algorithms (e.g., PBFT, RAFT) to enhance scalability and transaction speed, encryption protocols to ensure data privacy and selective visibility, and customizable frameworks to meet regulatory compliance in industries like finance and healthcare. Additionally, ICT facilitates interoperability through APIs and middleware, allowing seamless integration with legacy systems and other blockchains, while cloud computing and distributed ledger technologies provide the infrastructure for secure, efficient, and scalable enterprise solutions tailored to specific organizational needs.

Applications

Supply chain management, financial services, and healthcare.

Case Study

American Express created a private channel on a permissioned blockchain with each rewards merchant to facilitate information transfer, enhancing efficiency and security in their loyalty program.

Create Inquisitiveness and Curiosity

How can permissioned blockchains balance the need for privacy and regulatory compliance with the benefits of transparency and immutability?

Solved Problems

Design a basic consensus protocol for a permissioned blockchain with 12 nodes, where a Byzantine Fault Tolerance (BFT) of up to 4 faulty nodes is required. Suggest a suitable consensus algorithm and explain how it ensures agreement and fault tolerance.

Solution

PBFT (Practical Byzantine Fault Tolerance) would be a suitable algorithm. In PBFT, every node communicates with every other node to reach a consensus. The key condition for PBFT is that the number of faulty nodes (f) must be less than one-third of the total number of nodes (n), i.e., $f < (n-1)/3$.

In this case, we have n = 12 nodes and f = 4 faulty nodes. Check if the condition is met.

$4 < (12-1)/3$, which simplifies to $4 < 3.67$. This condition is not directly met for PBFT to operate perfectly because PBFT requires that $3f + 1 <= n$. With 4 faulty nodes, this becomes $3(4) + 1 <= 12$, which simplifies to $13 <= 12$, which is false.

However, for simpler understanding, it is often said that more than 2/3 of the nodes must be honest for PBFT to work effectively. PBFT achieves consensus through a series of steps, including pre-prepare, prepare, and commit phases. These phases ensure that all honest nodes agree on the same transaction order, even if up to 4 nodes are sending incorrect or malicious messages. The pre-prepare and prepare phases help to establish a common view of the proposed transaction, while the commit phase ensures that all nodes agree to execute the transaction.

2.5 CONSENSUS PROTOCOLS FOR PERMISSIONED BLOCKCHAINS

Permissioned blockchains typically employ consensus protocols that are more efficient and scalable than those used in public blockchains. Some of the key issues of permissioned blockchain is as given in figure 2.4.

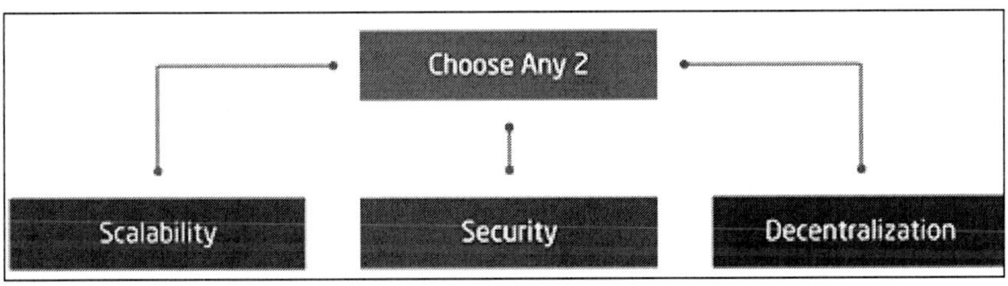

Figure 2.4: *Key Issues*

Some common consensus protocols for permissioned blockchains include:

- **Raft:** Raft is a consensus algorithm that is easy to understand and implement. It works by electing a leader who is responsible for coordinating the consensus process.

- **Paxos:** Paxos is a family of consensus protocols known for their fault tolerance. It is more complex than Raft but can tolerate a higher number of faulty nodes.
- **Practical Byzantine Fault Tolerance (PBFT):** PBFT is a consensus protocol designed for high-security environments. It can tolerate a certain number of malicious nodes in the network, making it suitable for applications where security is paramount. PBFT is well-suited for environments where there is a known group of participants, some of whom may be malicious or unreliable.

Video Resources
https://www.youtube.com/watch?v=3D8h5JLWKyo

Use of ICT

ICT plays a crucial role in implementing and managing consensus protocols for permissioned blockchains. It involves using software and hardware solutions to create, manage, and secure the blockchain network. For example, Trusted Execution Environments (TEEs) are used in consensus algorithms like PoET to ensure secure and efficient transaction validation.

Applications

- Supply Chain Management: Permissioned blockchains with consensus protocols like PBFT or RAFT can enhance supply chain transparency and efficiency by ensuring that all stakeholders agree on the state of goods and transactions.
- Financial Services: Banks and financial institutions use permissioned blockchains to securely and efficiently process transactions, leveraging consensus mechanisms to maintain trust and integrity.

Case Study

A notable case study is the use of Practical Byzantine Fault Tolerance (PBFT) in a permissioned blockchain for a financial institution. PBFT allows the network to tolerate up to one-third of faulty or malicious nodes, ensuring high fault tolerance and consistent performance. This consensus mechanism is particularly suited for environments requiring robust security and reliability, such as financial transactions.

Create Inquisitiveness and Curiosity

- How do permissioned blockchains ensure privacy and security while maintaining transparency?
- What are the advantages of using PBFT over other consensus mechanisms in permissioned blockchains?
- How can interoperability between different permissioned blockchain systems be improved?

Solved Problems

Problem 1: Byzantine Fault Tolerance in PBFT

Problem Statement: In a permissioned blockchain using Practical Byzantine Fault Tolerance (PBFT), if there are nnn nodes and up to f nodes can be faulty, what is the minimum number of nodes required to achieve consensus?

Solution: To achieve consensus, PBFT requires that at least 2f+1 nodes must be non-faulty. Therefore, the minimum number of nodes required is 3f+1,wheref is the maximum number of faulty nodes.

Mathematical Expression

$n \geq 3f+1$

Problem 2: Round Robin Consensus

Problem Statement: In a round robin consensus protocol, if there are n validators and each validator takes t time units to validate a block, what is the total time required to validate a block if all validators must validate it sequentially?

Solution:

The total time required is the sum of the validation times for all validators, which is:

$T = n \times t$

SUMMARY

- Consensus protocols are vital for agreement in distributed systems, with key requirements including agreement, termination, integrity, and fault tolerance.
- Proof of Work (PoW) is a foundational consensus mechanism that requires computational effort to validate transactions and secure the blockchain.
- Scalability remains a significant challenge for blockchain consensus protocols, leading to the development of alternative mechanisms and scaling solutions.
- Permissioned blockchains have distinct design goals and utilize consensus protocols that prioritize access control, privacy, and regulatory compliance.

EXERCISES

A. Subjective Questions

Category-I *(Revised Bloom's Level-1, 2 & 3)*

- List and briefly describe the key requirements of a consensus protocol. (Level 1)
- Explain how Proof of Work (PoW) achieves consensus in a decentralized network. (Level 2)
- Compare the advantages and disadvantages of Proof of Work (PoW) and Proof of Stake (PoS). (Level 3)

Category-II *(Revised Bloom's Level-4, 5 & 6)*

- Analyze the trade-offs involved in choosing a consensus protocol for a specific blockchain application. (Level 4)
- Evaluate the suitability of different consensus protocols for a permissioned blockchain scenario. (Level 5)
- Design a novel consensus mechanism that addresses the limitations of existing protocols. (Level 6)

B. Objective Questions

Category-I ***(Revised Bloom's Level-1, 2 & 3)***

- Which of the following is a core requirement of a consensus protocol?

  (a) Speed (b) Agreement

  (c) Cost (d) Complexity (Level 1)

- What is the primary function of Proof of Work (PoW) in a blockchain? (Level 2)

  (a) Smart contract execution (b) Transaction validation

  (c) Data storage (d) Encryption

- Which of these is a benefit of Proof of Work (PoW)?(Level 3)

  (a) Energy efficiency (b) Scalability

  (c) Decentralization (d) Low cost

Category-II ***(Revised Bloom's Level-4, 5 & 6)***

- For an enterprise blockchain requiring high throughput and Byzantine fault tolerance, which consensus protocol would be most appropriate? Justify your answer. (Level 5)

TEACHER'S KNOW MORE

- Research the latest advances in consensus algorithms, including hybrid approaches and directed acyclic graphs (DAGs).
- Investigate the security vulnerabilities of different consensus protocols and potential mitigation strategies.
- Explore the evolving regulatory landscape surrounding blockchain technology and its impact on consensus protocol design.

UNIT 3

Hyperledger Fabric

RATIONALE

This unit introduces Hyperledger Fabric, an enterprise-grade distributed ledger technology crucial for building permissioned blockchain solutions. Understanding its architecture, components, and consensus mechanisms is essential for developing secure, scalable, and private blockchain applications tailored to various industries, including supply chain, finance, and healthcare. This unit provides a comprehensive overview of Hyperledger Fabric, its key features, and its practical applications.

OUTCOMES

- Understand the architecture and key features of Hyperledger Fabric.
- Describe the consensus process and its components in Hyperledger Fabric.
- Explain the role of chaincode in Hyperledger Fabric and its design principles.
- Explore advanced functionalities beyond chaincode, such as Fabric Private Chaincode and decentralized governance.

3.1 HYPERLEDGER FABRIC (A): DECOMPOSING THE CONSENSUS PROCESS

Hyperledger Fabric's modular consensus allows organizations to choose algorithms like Solo, Kafka, or Raft.

3.1.1 Introduction to Hyperledger Fabric

Hyperledger Fabric is an open-source, enterprise-grade distributed ledger technology (DLT) platform designed for use in business contexts.

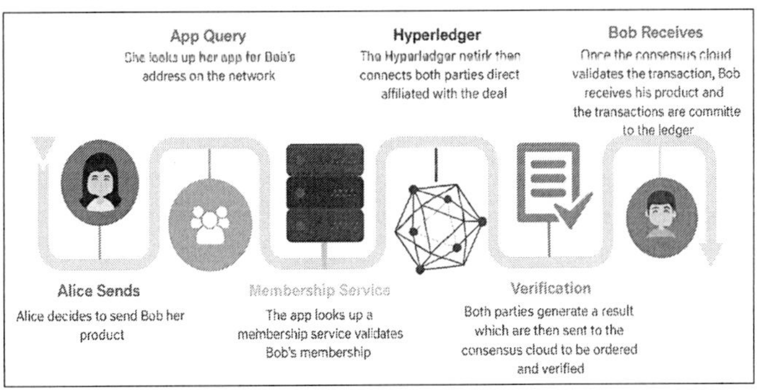

Figure 3.1: Basics of Hyperledger

Developed under the Linux Foundation, it provides a modular architecture enabling organizations to create customizable blockchain solutions tailored to their specific needs. Unlike traditional public blockchains, Hyperledger Fabric is permissioned, meaning that all participants are known and verified, which is crucial for industries that require stringent data privacy and compliance measures.

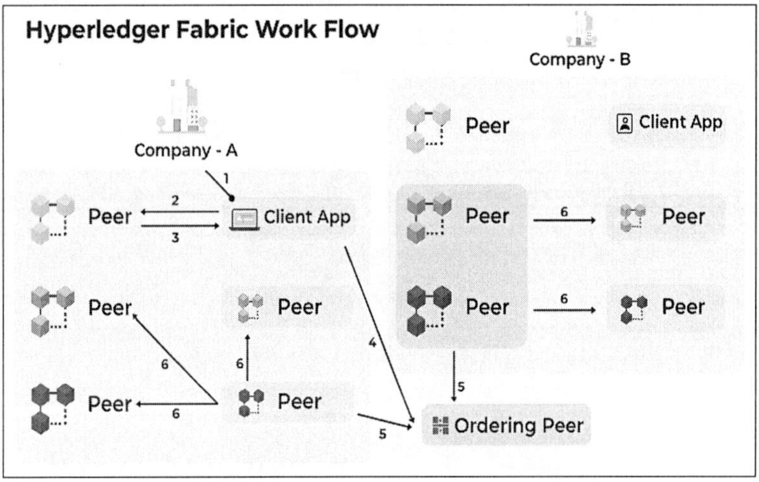

Figure 3.2: *Hyperledger Fabric Work Flow*

3.1.2 Key Features of Hyperledger Fabric

- **Modular Architecture:** Hyperledger Fabric's architecture is highly modular, allowing organizations to plug in various components as needed.
  - ✓ **Consensus Mechanisms:** Organizations can choose from multiple consensus algorithms like Solo, Kafka, or Raft, depending on their needs for fault tolerance and performance.
  - ✓ **Membership Services:** A pluggable membership service provider (MSP) manages identities and permissions, ensuring that only authorized participants can access the network.
  - ✓ **Chaincode (Smart Contracts):** Smart contracts in Hyperledger Fabric are referred to as chaincode and can be written in standard programming languages such as Go and JavaScript. This flexibility makes it easier for developers to implement business logic.
- **Privacy and Confidentiality:** Hyperledger Fabric supports private transactions through the use of channels. Channels allow a subset of network participants to create a separate ledger where transactions can occur privately.
- **Performance and Scalability:** The transaction model in Hyperledger Fabric follows an execute-order-commit approach. This means that transactions are first executed by peers, then ordered, and finally committed to the ledger.

3.1.3 Overview of Consensus in Hyperledger Fabric

Consensus in Hyperledger Fabric is not merely about agreeing on the order of transactions; it encompasses the entire lifecycle of a transaction, from proposal to commitment. The consensus mechanism is designed to ensure that all participants in the network agree on the state of the ledger while maintaining privacy and security.

i **Endorsement Phase**: The endorsement phase is where the transaction proposal is created and validated by designated endorsing peers. Here's how it works:

- **Transaction Proposal:** A client application generates a transaction proposal and sends it to one or more endorsing peers.
- **Validation:** Each endorsing peer checks
  - ✓ The proposal format is correct.
  - ✓ The transaction has not been submitted previously.
  - ✓ The cryptographic signature is valid.
  - ✓ The client has authorization to perform the operation.

- **Execution:** The endorsing peers simulate the transaction by executing it against their current state of the ledger (world state) using chaincode (smart contracts). This execution generates a read/write set that reflects what data would be read and written if the transaction were to be committed.
- **Endorsement Policy:** Each transaction must meet a predefined endorsement policy, typically requiring signatures from multiple peers (e.g., "m out of n" signatures) before it can proceed to the next phase

ii **Ordering Phase:**Once a transaction has received sufficient endorsements, it moves to the ordering phase:

- **Ordering Service:** The endorsed transactions are sent to an ordering service, which organizes them into a block. Hyperledger Fabric supports various consensus algorithms for ordering, including:
- **Solo:** A single node orders transactions; suitable for development but not production.
- **Kafka:** A crash fault-tolerant mechanism where only a leader node orders transactions, ensuring quick finality but lacking Byzantine fault tolerance.

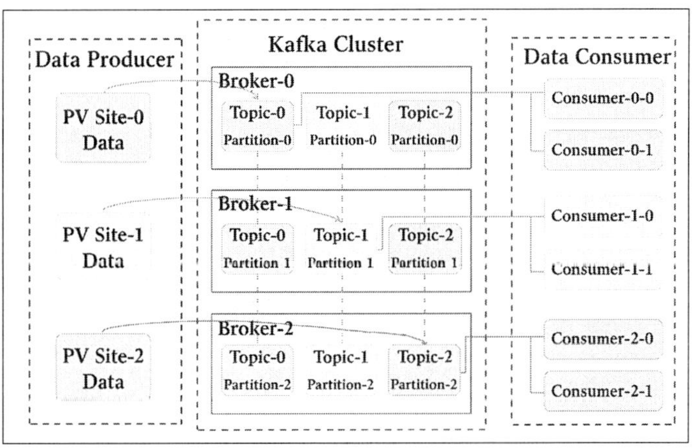

***Figure 3.3:** Kafka Framework in three replicas mode*

- **Raft:** A leader/follower consensus algorithm used in later versions, which provides crash fault tolerance.

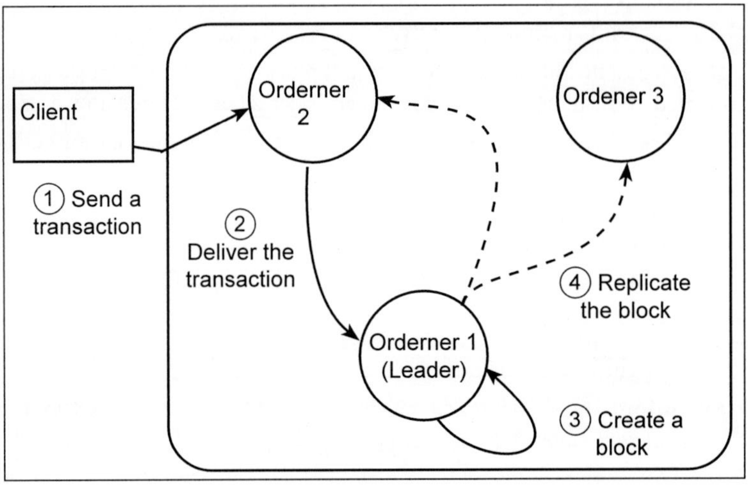

Figure 3.4: *Raft operation in Hyperledger Fabric*

The ordering service ensures that all nodes receive transactions in the same order, which is essential for maintaining consistency across the network.

i **Validation Phase:** The final phase involves validating and committing the ordered transactions:

- **Validation Process:** Each peer receives blocks of ordered transactions from the ordering service. During this phase, each peer performs several checks:
  - ✓ Verifies that each transaction meets its endorsement policy.
  - ✓ Checks that read/write sets are valid using multi-version concurrency control (MVCC) to prevent conflicts with concurrent transactions.
- **Commitment:** Valid transactions are then committed to the ledger. Each peer updates its local copy of the world state based on the write sets from valid transactions.

Video Resources
Hyperledger Ordering Service: Deep Dive into the Raft Consensus Algorithm

Use of ICT

Hyperledger Fabric provides flexible tools for configuring and monitoring consensus mechanisms, particularly when using the Raft ordering service. Here's how to manage these processes through CLI tools and dashboards.

Configuring Consensus Mechanisms

1. Setting up Raft via CLI

Initialize a 5-node Raft network using Fabric's `byfn.sh` script:

bash

```
./byfn.sh generate -o etcdraft
./byfn.sh up -o etcdraft
```

This creates separate Docker containers for each ordering node with crash fault tolerance.

2. Modifying Channel Configurations

To migrate from Kafka to Raft:

- Enter maintenance mode:

  bash

  peer channel update -f config_update.pb -c mychannel -o orderer.example.com:7050

- Update `configtx.yaml` to specify `ConsensusType: etcdraft` and add Raft node details.

3. Dynamic Node Management

Add/remove ordering nodes using channel configuration updates:

bash

configtxlator proto_encode --input modified_config.json --type common.Config --output config.pb

peer channel signconfigtx -f config.pb

Monitoring Consensus Operations

1. CLI-Based Monitoring

- Check block commit status:

  bash

  peer channel getinfo -c mychannel

- View ordering node logs:

  bash

  docker logs -f orderer.example.com

2. Dashboard Integration

Metric Type	Tools	Key Indicators
Performance	Prometheus + Grafana	Block latency, Tx throughput
Security	Splunk App for Hyperledger	Orphaned blocks, Leader changes
Blockchain Health	Hyperledger Explorer	Channel activity, Node status

3. Consensus-Specific Alerts

- Monitor leader elections via Prometheus metrics:

  bash

  raft_leader_changes_total

- Detect configuration changes in Splunk using `chaincode_instantiate` or `config_update` events.

For production environments, combine CLI checks with dashboard visualizations to track consensus stability and detect anomalies like prolonged leader elections or unexpected channel reconfigurations.

Applications (Real Life/Industrial)

- Supply Chain Management: It enhances traceability and transparency by allowing organizations to track goods from origin to destination.
- Financial Services: The platform supports secure transactions and compliance with regulatory standards.
- Healthcare: It facilitates secure sharing of patient data while maintaining privacy.

Case-Study (Environmental/Sustainability/Social/Ethical Issues)

Walmart's implementation of Hyperledger Fabric for food supply chain transparency offers a foundational model for creating auditable, sustainable material sourcing systems. Here's an adapted case study showcasing how similar principles can be applied to sustainable materials.

Sustainable Timber Tracking Initiative

- **Industry:** Forestry & Manufacturing
- **Technology:** Hyperledger Fabric
- **Partners:** Global Forestry Consortium, IBM

Challenge

A coalition of 15 forestry companies faced mounting pressure to prove ethical sourcing of timber products. Traditional paper-based systems allowed:

- 7-10 day verification times for wood origin
- 18% error rate in sustainability certification tracking
- No real-time visibility into subcontractor compliance

Solution

The consortium deployed a Hyperledger Fabric blockchain network with:

1. **Smart Contracts** for automatic certification validation
2. **IoT Integration**

- GPS trackers on logging trucks
- QR codes linking timber batches to forest origin

1. **Multi-organization Channels**

- Separate private channels for competitors' proprietary data
- Shared sustainability compliance ledger

Key Technical Implementation

```
bash
# Node.js chaincode for certification checks
async validateCert(ctx, batchId){
const cert = await ctx.stub.getState(batchId);
if(!cert|| cert.owner !== ctx.clientIdentity.getID()){
throw new Error('Invalid sustainability certification');
```

```
}
return cert;
}
```

Results

Metric	Before Fabric	After Fabric
Certification Verification	14 days	8 seconds
Audit Preparation Time	45 staff-hours	3 staff-hours
Illegal Logging Incidents	22/yr	3/yr

The system now tracks 300K+ timber batches annually across 7 countries. Regulatory auditors receive real-time API access to

- Chain-of-custody records
- Sustainability certification updates
- Carbon footprint calculations at each processing stage

Supply Chain Impact

- 89% reduction in certification fraud attempts
- 40% faster customs clearance for verified sustainable shipments
- First blockchain-validated "Conflict-Free Timber" label issued in 2024

This model adapts Walmart's Fabric implementation principles to sustainable materials, leveraging:

1. **Modular Consensus:** Raft protocol handles 1500+ TPS for high-volume logging operations
2. **Privacy Features:** Zero-knowledge proofs hide proprietary supplier pricing while validating sustainability metrics
3. **Multi-org Governance:** Voting system for certificate standard updates using Fabric's dynamic configuration

As demonstrated in the Walmart food case, Fabric's permissioned structure enables collaboration between competitors while maintaining data confidentiality – critical for industry-wide sustainability efforts. The system's success has prompted expansion to rare earth mineral tracking, with 8 mining firms joining the network in Q1 2025.

Create Inquisitiveness and Curiosity

How does Hyperledger Fabric's consensus mechanism compare to proof-of-work or proof-of-stake used in public blockchains?

Solved Problems (With Increasing Difficulty Level)

- **Basic:** Configuring a simple Hyperledger Fabric network with the Solo consensus.
- **Intermediate:** Implementing an endorsement policy requiring multiple organizations to endorse a transaction.
- **Advanced:** Analyzing and resolving MVCC_READ_CONFLICT errors in a high-concurrency environment.

3.2 HYPERLEDGER FABRIC COMPONENTS

Hyperledger Fabric's modularity allows components to be upgraded or replaced without disrupting the entire network.

3.2.1 Core Components of Hyperledger Fabric

- **Distributed Ledger:** Records all data about transactions, ensuring transparency and traceability.
- **Peers (Nodes):** Maintain the ledger and execute chaincode (smart contracts). Peer nodes endorse transactions, execute smart contracts (Chaincode), and store a local copy of the ledger.
- **Smart Contracts (Chaincode):** Contain the application logic. They process the distributed logic and agreement of the system.
- **Consensus (Endorsement):** Transactions must be ratified by a consensus of nodes entered into the ledger; in Fabric, this is referred to as an endorsement.
- **Membership Service Provider (MSP):** Defines the rules in which identities are validated, authenticated, and allowed access to a network. The MSP manages user IDs and authenticates clients who want to join the network. It issues certificates for users and manages permissions.
- **Client:** Submits transaction proposals through the Fabric SDK.
- **Orderer:** Orders transactions in ascending order and forms a block. The ordering service ensures that transactions are properly ordered and broadcasts new blocks to peer nodes.
- **Assets:** Represented as a sequence of key-value pairs and can range from tangible to intangible.
- **Certificate Authorities (CA):** Connect the whole network via certificate's chain of trust.

Video Resources
What Is Hyperledger Fabric And How It Works? | Hyperledger Fabric Tutorial | Simplilearn

Use of ICT

Using tools like Hyperledger Explorer to visualize the ledger and monitor network activity.

Applications (Real Life/Industrial)

- Supply chain: Tracking assets and verifying their provenance.
- Healthcare: Managing patient records securely and privately.

Case-Study (Environmental/Sustainability/Social/Ethical Issues)

A case study on using Hyperledger Fabric for a carbon credit trading platform.

Create Inquisitiveness and Curiosity

How does the MSP ensure that only authorized participants can access the network?

Solved Problems (With Increasing Difficulty Level)

- **Basic:** Setting up a basic Hyperledger Fabric network with one peer and one orderer.
- **Intermediate:** Configuring the MSP to manage identities and permissions for different organizations.
- **Advanced:** Troubleshooting network issues related to certificate expiration or invalid MSP configurations.

3.3 CHAINCODE DESIGN AND IMPLEMENTATION IN HYPERLEDGER

Chaincode can be written in multiple languages, including Go, Java, and Node.js.

3.3.1 Chaincode Design and Implementation in Hyperledger:

Chaincode, often referred to as smart contracts in other blockchain platforms, is a fundamental component of Hyperledger Fabric. It encapsulates the business logic that governs the interactions with the ledger. Figure 3.5 shows the chaincode execution model.

***Figure 3.5:** Chaincode Execution Model*

Here's a detailed overview of best practices and guidelines for designing and implementing chaincode in Hyperledger Fabric.

Development Environment

- ✓ **Use Chaincode DevMode:** This mode allows for easier debugging and testing during development.
- ✓ **Logging:** Utilize Hyperledger Fabric's built-in logging mechanisms to track chaincode execution and errors. For example
  - **Golang:** Use github.com/hyperledger/fabric/core/chaincode/shim#ChaincodeLogger.
  - **NodeJS:** Use fabric-shim for logging.
  - **Java:** Implement any standard logging framework like Log4J.

Writing Deterministic Chaincode

Ensure that your chaincode is deterministic, meaning it should produce the same output given the same input regardless of the environment or time of execution. Avoid using non-deterministic functions such as:

- rand.New(...)
- time.Now()

This is crucial because non-deterministic chaincode can lead to endorsement policy failures during validation.

Handling State and Transactions

- ✓ **Optimistic Locking Model:** Hyperledger Fabric employs an optimistic locking model, which can lead to MVCC_READ_CONFLICT errors if concurrent transactions attempt to modify the same key. Ensure that your chaincode handles potential conflicts gracefully.
- ✓ **Avoid Global Keys:** Instead of relying on global state, use local variables or parameters within your functions to minimize conflicts.
- **Efficient Use of CouchDB:** When using CouchDB as the state database, be aware that queries do not alter the read set of a transaction. This means you should structure your data to optimize query performance without impacting transaction integrity.Store keys as properties within your data models rather than querying by key names directly.

Structuring Chaincode

Define clear data structures for assets or entities you are managing on the ledger. For example:

```
go
type Asset struct{
ID  string`json:"id"`
Name string`json:"name"`
// Additional fields
}
```

Implement functions for asset management (e.g., create, read, update, delete) that adhere to best practices in error handling and state management.

Testing and Validation

Rigorously test your chaincode before deployment. Utilize unit tests to ensure that each function behaves as expected under various scenarios.Consider using tools like Hyperledger Caliper for performance testing.

Upgrading Chaincode

When upgrading chaincode, ensure backward compatibility with existing ledger states. The upgraded chaincode should be able to handle both old and new data definitions seamlessly.

> **Video Resources**
> After 3 Years of Gap, How she got a Package of 15 LPA | Nisha's Success Story | Be10x Review

Use of ICT

Using IDEs and debugging tools to develop and test chaincode.

Applications (Real Life/Industrial)

- Finance: Automating financial agreements and transactions.
- Insurance: Processing insurance claims automatically.

Case-Study (Environmental/Sustainability/Social/Ethical Issues)

Developing chaincode for tracking and verifying carbon offsets.

Create Inquisitiveness and Curiosity

How can chaincode be designed to handle complex business logic and interactions between different parties?

Solved Problems (With Increasing Difficulty Level)

- **Basic:** Writing a simple chaincode to create and transfer assets.
- **Intermediate:** Handling concurrent transactions and resolving MVCC_READ_CONFLICT errors.
- **Advanced:** Implementing a complex chaincode with multiple functions and dependencies on external libraries.

3.4 FABRIC (B): BEYOND CHAINCODE

Fabric Private Chaincode (FPC) uses Intel SGX to ensure that sensitive data remains confidential. While chaincode is a fundamental aspect of Hyperledger Fabric, enabling the execution of smart contracts and business logic, there are several advanced functionalities and components that extend the capabilities of Hyperledger Fabric beyond just chaincode.

Fabric Private Chaincode (FPC)

Fabric Private Chaincode as shown in figure 3.6 allows for the execution of chaincodes within a secure environment using Intel Software Guard Extensions (SGX). This ensures that sensitive data and computations remain confidential, even from potentially untrusted peers in the network.

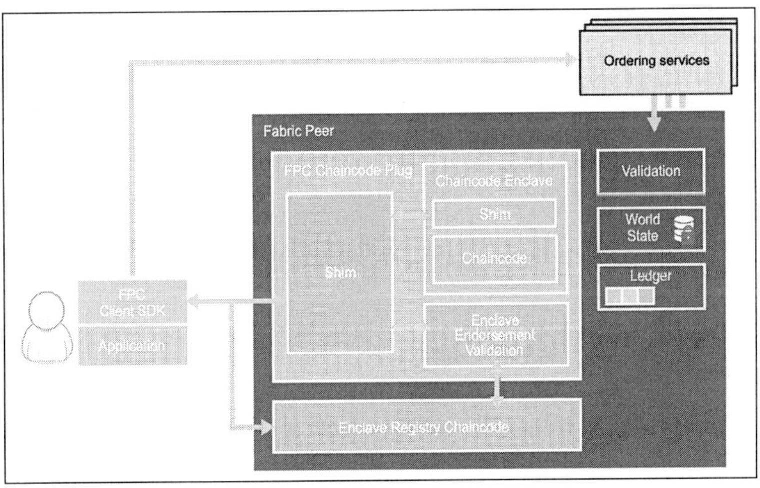

Figure 3.6: *Fabric Private Chaincode*

FPC introduces a chaincode enclave that isolates the execution of chaincode from the peer node. It includes components such as:

- ✓ **Enclave Registry:** Maintains identities of all chaincode enclaves and performs attestation to verify their integrity.
- ✓ **Enclave Endorsement Validation:** Validates transactions produced by the chaincode enclave before they are committed to the ledger.
- ✓ **Benefits:** This approach enhances privacy by encrypting data on the ledger and allowing only authorized parties to access it in clear form, thus addressing confidentiality concerns in blockchain applications.

Chaincode as an External Service

- ✓ **Deployment Flexibility:** Starting from Fabric v2.0, chaincode can be deployed and executed outside of Fabric's peer nodes. This allows for independent management of the chaincode lifecycle, particularly useful in cloud environments like Kubernetes.
- ✓ **Service Management:** By running chaincode as an external service, organizations can streamline deployment processes, reduce resource consumption on peers, and enhance scalability.

Chaincode-to-Chaincode Invocation

- ✓ **Inter-Chaincode Communication:** Hyperledger Fabric supports invoking one chaincode from another. This feature enables complex interactions and workflows across different chaincodes within the network.
- ✓ **Considerations:** When invoking chaincodes across different channels, keep in mind that such calls are treated as queries and do not participate in state validation during the commit phase. This capability is essential for building modular applications where functionality can be reused.
- **Decentralized Governance for Smart Contracts**
- ✓ **Governance Model:** Hyperledger Fabric v2.x as given in figure 3.7 introduces a decentralized governance model for managing smart contracts (chaincode). This allows multiple organizations within a network to collaboratively decide on parameters related to chaincode operation.

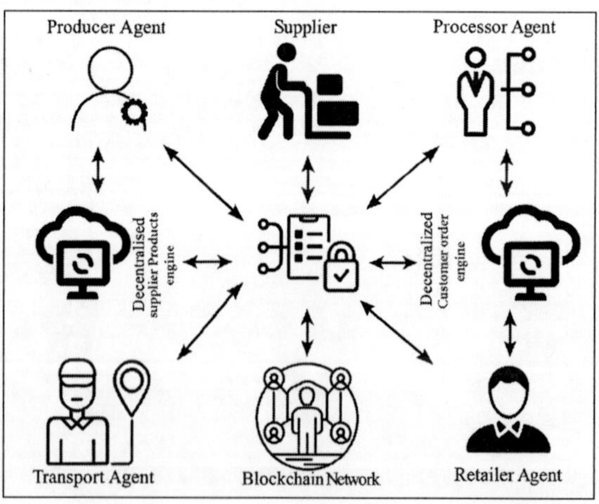

Figure 3.7: *Decentralized Smart Contract Based Supply Chain*

✓ **Lifecycle Management:** The new lifecycle process provides mechanisms for managing approvals, upgrades, and versioning of chaincodes across different organizations, ensuring that all stakeholders have a say in how their shared resources are managed.

Integration with REST APIs

✓ **API Development:** Developers can create RESTful APIs to facilitate communication between client applications (like mobile apps) and Hyperledger Fabric networks. This is achieved using SDKs available for various programming languages (e.g., Java SDK).

✓ **Use Cases:** REST APIs enable external applications to interact with the blockchain seamlessly, allowing for broader integration with existing systems and enhancing user experience.

Video Resources
Integrating Fabric Private Chaincode with Hyperledger CC-Tools

Use of ICT

Using tools to deploy and manage chaincode as external services in a cloud environment.

Applications (Real Life/Industrial)

- **Healthcare:** Securely sharing patient data with authorized parties.
- **Finance:** Protecting sensitive financial data from unauthorized access.

Case-Study (Environmental/Sustainability/Social/Ethical Issues)

Using decentralized governance to manage a supply chain for ethically sourced goods.

Create Inquisitiveness and Curiosity

How does Fabric's decentralized governance model ensure that all stakeholders have a say in managing shared resources?

Solved Problems (With Increasing Difficulty Level)

- **Basic:** Setting up and configuring FPC for a simple chaincode.
- **Intermediate:** Implementing chaincode-to chaincode invocation across different channels.
- **Advanced:** Developing a REST API to interact with a Hyperledger Fabric network and manage user authentication.

3.5 FABRIC SDK AND FRONT END

To integrate a front-end application with Hyperledger Fabric, developers typically utilize the Hyperledger Fabric SDKs, which facilitate communication between the front end and the blockchain network. Here's a structured overview of how to achieve this integration.

3.5.1 Overview of Hyperledger Fabric SDKs

Hyperledger Fabric provides several SDKs for different programming languages, including

- **Node.js SDK**: As given in figure 3.8 is ideal for JavaScript applications, commonly used in web development.

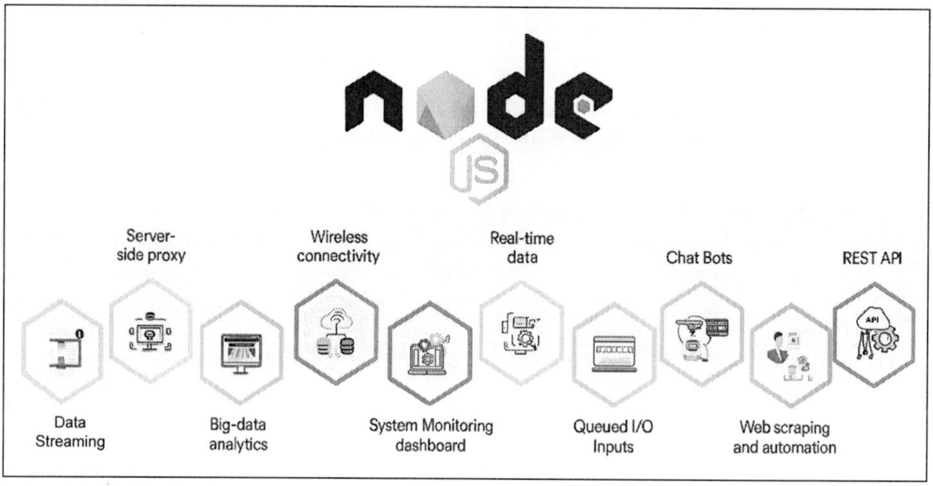

***Figure 3.8:** The history of Node.js*

- **Java SDK**: Suitable for Java applications, allowing for robust enterprise solutions.
- **Go SDK**: Primarily used for backend services and chaincode development.

These SDKs allow developers to interact with the Fabric network by submitting transactions, querying the ledger, and managing identities.

3.5.2 Setting Up the Backend

To connect a front-end application with Hyperledger Fabric, it is common to create a backend service that uses the Fabric SDK. Here's how to set it up.

- **Install Dependencies**: Use Node.js for the backend. Install the necessary packages using npm: npm install fabric-network
- **Create Connection Profile**: This profile contains information about the network configuration, including peers, orderers, and certificate authorities (CAs). Export this from your Hyperledger Fabric network setup.
- **Implement API Endpoints**: Create RESTful API endpoints in your backend application that will handle requests from the front end and interact with the blockchain using the SDK. For example:
  - ✓ **Submit Transaction**: An endpoint to submit transactions to the blockchain.
  - ✓ **Query Ledger**: An endpoint to retrieve data from the ledger.

3.5.3 Front-End Integration

Once your backend is set up and can communicate with Hyperledger Fabric, you can create a front-end application that interacts with this backend.

- **Framework Choice**: You can use frameworks like Angular, React, or Vue.js for building your front end.
- **API Calls**: Use HTTP requests (e.g., using Axios or Fetch API) to call your backend API endpoints.

  For example:

  ```
  axios.post('http://localhost:4000/submitTransaction', { data })
  .then(response => {
  console.log('Transaction submitted:', response.data);
  })
  .catch(error => {
  console.error('Error submitting transaction:', error);
  });
  ```
- **User Interface**: Design forms and components to capture user input for transactions and display results retrieved from the blockchain.

3.5.4 Example Workflow

a. **User Interaction**: The user interacts with the front end (e.g., filling out a form).
b. **API Request**: The front end sends an API request to the backend.
c. **Chaincode Invocation**: The backend uses the Fabric SDK to invoke chaincode or query the ledger.
d. **Response Handling**: The backend sends back a response to the front end, which updates the UI accordingly.

3.5.5 Deployment Considerations

- Ensure that both your front-end and back-end applications are deployed in environments where they can securely communicate with each other.
- Use HTTPS for secure communication between clients and servers.
- Manage user identities securely by implementing wallet management in your backend.

Integrating a front-end application with Hyperledger Fabric involves setting up a backend service using one of the available Fabric SDKs and creating a user-friendly interface that communicates with this service. By following these steps, developers can create robust decentralized applications that leverage blockchain technology effectively.

Video Resources
https://www.youtube.com/watch?v=jtP403_CYzY

Use of ICT

Using Information and Communication Technology (ICT) for Hyperledger Fabric SDK and front-end development involves leveraging various tools and technologies to build blockchain applications.

ICT in Hyperledger Fabric SDK

1. **Programming Languages**: Hyperledger Fabric provides SDKs for multiple programming languages such as **Node.js**, **Java**, and **Go**. These SDKs enable developers to interact with the blockchain network programmatically, allowing them to create, deploy, and manage smart contracts (chaincode) and perform transactions.
2. **Blockchain Network Setup**: ICT tools like Docker and Kubernetes are used to set up and manage Fabric networks. Docker provides containerization for Fabric components like peers and orderers, while Kubernetes can be used for orchestration.
3. **Certificate Authority (CA)**: Fabric CA is used for identity management and authentication within the network. It issues certificates to users and organizations, ensuring secure interactions.

ICT for Front-end Development

1. **Web Applications**: Front-end frameworks like **React**, **Angular**, or **Vue.js** can be used to build user interfaces for blockchain applications. These interfaces interact with the Fabric network via the SDKs, allowing users to perform transactions or query the blockchain.
2. **API Integration**: RESTful APIs can be created using Node.js or other backend technologies to act as intermediaries between the front-end and the Fabric network. This allows for secure and controlled access to blockchain data and functionality.
3. **Security Measures**: ICT tools and practices, such as encryption and secure authentication protocols (e.g., TLS), are essential for ensuring the security of data transmitted between the front-end and the Fabric network.

Applications (Real Life/Industrial)

- **Asset Transfer Application**: An application built using the Fabric SDK for Node.js can interact with a deployed blockchain network. The front-end, developed with React, allows users to transfer assets securely by invoking smart contracts through the Fabric network.

Case-Study (Environmental/Sustainability/Social/Ethical Issues)

Supply Chain Management Application Using Hyperledger Fabric SDK and Front-End Integration

A leading logistics company faced inefficiencies in tracking shipments and ensuring transparency across its supply chain network. To address these challenges, the company implemented a blockchain-based solution using **Hyperledger Fabric SDK** and a custom-built front-end application. The backend leveraged Fabric's permissioned blockchain to create a secure and decentralized network where suppliers, manufacturers, and distributors could interact transparently. Using the Fabric SDK for Node.js, the company developed smart contracts to automate processes such as shipment tracking, inventory updates, and compliance checks. The front-end application, built with React.js, provided an intuitive interface for stakeholders to query shipment statuses, submit transactions, and receive real-time notifications about delays or updates. This integration ensured secure data exchange, improved accountability, and reduced operational costs by eliminating manual reconciliation processes. The modular design of Hyperledger Fabric also allowed the company to scale the network as new partners joined the ecosystem.

Create Inquisitiveness and Curiosity

Let's spark some curiosity and inquisitiveness about using Hyperledger Fabric SDK and front-end integration for blockchain applications.

Questions to Ponder

1. How can blockchain technology revolutionize industries like supply chain management, healthcare, or finance?
2. Imagine a world where transactions are transparent, tamper-proof, and secure. How would this change the way businesses operate?
3. What are the potential benefits of integrating a blockchain network with a user-friendly front-end application?
4. Think about how a seamless user interface could make complex blockchain interactions accessible to a broader audience.
5. How does Hyperledger Fabric's permissioned blockchain model ensure security and privacy in a decentralized network?
6. Consider the importance of controlling who can access and modify data in a blockchain ecosystem.
7. What role do smart contracts play in automating processes within a blockchain application?
8. Explore how these self-executing contracts with the terms of the agreement directly written into lines of code can streamline operations.
9. How can developers leverage the Fabric SDK to build scalable and efficient blockchain applications?
10. Delve into the tools and features provided by the SDK that make it easier to develop, deploy, and manage blockchain solutions.

Curiosity-Driven Activities

- **Experiment with a Simple Blockchain Application**: Try building a basic blockchain app using Hyperledger Fabric and a front-end framework like React. This hands-on experience can help you understand the concepts better.
- **Read Case Studies**: Look for real-world examples of companies that have successfully implemented blockchain solutions using Hyperledger Fabric. Analyze their challenges, solutions, and outcomes.
- **Join Online Communities**: Participate in forums or discussion groups focused on blockchain development. Engage with experts and enthusiasts to learn more about the latest trends and innovations.
- **Attend Webinars or Workshops**: Attend online sessions or workshops that cover topics related to blockchain development with Hyperledger Fabric. These events often provide valuable insights and networking opportunities.

Thought-Provoking Scenarios

- **Imagine a Blockchain-Based Voting System**: How could Hyperledger Fabric be used to create a secure, transparent, and tamper-proof voting system? What would be the benefits and challenges of such a system?
- **Envision a Decentralized Social Media Platform**: How might a blockchain-based social media platform, built using Hyperledger Fabric and a user-friendly front-end, change the way we interact online? What privacy and security features could it offer?

Solved Problems (With Increasing Difficulty Level)

1. Basic Problem: Connecting Front-End to Hyperledger Fabric

Problem: How to connect a front-end application (e.g., React or Angular) to a Hyperledger Fabric network?

Solution: Use a web service as an intermediary between the front-end and the Fabric network. The front-end sends requests to the web service, which interacts with the Fabric network using the Node.js SDK. For example:

- Use the `contract.submitTransaction` API from the SDK to invoke smart contracts.
- **Example frameworks:** Vue.js or Angular for UI, Node.js for backend interaction.

2. Intermediate Problem: Implementing User Authentication

Problem: How to implement user registration and login in a blockchain-based application?

Solution: Use Hyperledger Fabric's Certificate Authority (CA) for identity management. Users register and enroll via the CA, and their credentials are stored securely in wallets on the server-side. The front-end interacts with this setup through REST APIs.

- **Example:** Create a registration page where users submit details, which are passed to the backend for enrollment using Fabric's CA API.

3. Advanced Problem: Direct Front-End Interaction with Fabric

Problem: Is it possible to connect directly from a React front-end to a Hyperledger Fabric network?

Solution: While direct connection is challenging due to gRPC and HTTP/2 protocols, you can use Fabric Gateway APIs with offline signing. This ensures that private keys remain on the client-side while the server handles transaction submission securely.

- Implement "offline signing" where the server sends unsigned messages to the client for signing, ensuring minimal exposure of sensitive data.

4. Expert Problem: Optimizing Performance and Scalability

Problem: How to scale a Hyperledger Fabric application while maintaining performance?

Solution: Optimize key components:

- Use LevelDB for simple key-value storage or CouchDB for complex queries.
- Choose efficient endorsement policies and minimize endorsing nodes.

- Use Go or Java for chaincode development instead of JavaScript for better performance.
- Deploy in Kubernetes clusters with sufficient resources (e.g., SSDs, high-memory nodes).

3.6 HYPERLEDGER COMPOSER TOOL

Hyperledger Composer as given in figure 3.9 is an open development toolset and framework designed to simplify the creation of blockchain applications on the Hyperledger Fabric platform. It accelerates the development process, enabling developers and business analysts to collaborate effectively in building and deploying blockchain solutions.

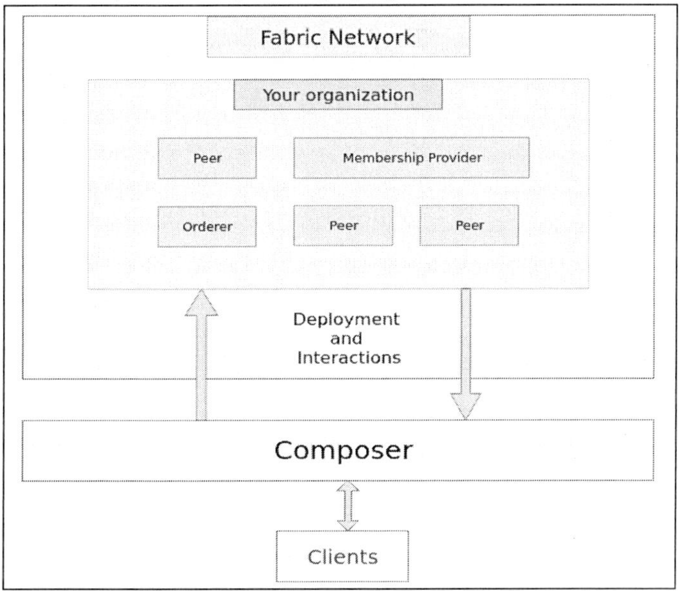

Figure 3.9: *Composer in a Hyperledger Fabric Development*

3.6.1 Key Components of Hyperledger Composer

1. **Execution Runtimes**: These are environments where the business logic defined in Composer is executed, typically on Hyperledger Fabric.
2. **JavaScript SDK**: A set of Node.js APIs that allow developers to interact with and manage business networks. It includes:
   - **Composer-admin**: For managing business networks (installing, upgrading, starting).
   - **Composer-client**: For performing operations like creating, reading, updating, and deleting assets and participants.
3. **Command Line Interface (CLI):** The Composer CLI provides essential command-line tools for deploying and managing business networks. It supports various administrative and operational tasks.
4. **REST Server**: This component exposes the blockchain's assets, participants, and transactions through a RESTful API, enabling integration with web or mobile applications.

5. **LoopBack Connector**: Facilitates integration with existing enterprise systems by allowing various client applications to interface with the blockchain.
6. **Playground Web User Interface**: A web-based interface for defining, testing, and prototyping business networks without requiring local installations. It allows users to visualize network structures and interactions.
7. **Yeoman Code Generator**: Utilizes the Yeoman framework to create skeleton projects for Angular web applications, Node.js applications, and business networks quickly.
8. **VSCode and Atom Editor Plugins**: Extensions that provide syntax highlighting, error detection, and snippets support for developing Composer models and access control lists (ACLs).

3.6.2 Features of Hyperledger Composer

- **Simple Modeling Language**: Composer uses JavaScript for defining business networks, making it accessible to developers familiar with this language.
- **Rapid Prototyping**: The tool enables quick development cycles, allowing teams to build proof-of-concept applications efficiently.
- **Integration Capabilities**: It facilitates seamless integration with existing systems through its REST API and LoopBack connectors.
- **Access Control Management**: Composer allows for defining roles and access controls for participants within the blockchain network.

3.6.3 Use Cases

Hyperledger Composer is particularly useful in scenarios where businesses need to model complex interactions among participants while ensuring secure access to data. For example:

- A real estate application can use Composer to model properties as assets, buyers as participants, and transactions for buying or selling properties.
- Integration with existing inventory systems can automate the addition of new assets (houses) and removal of sold properties from the ledger.

Hyperledger Composer serves as a powerful toolset that simplifies the development of blockchain applications on Hyperledger Fabric. By providing a comprehensive framework that includes various components for modeling, testing, and integrating blockchain solutions, it enables organizations to accelerate their blockchain initiatives while ensuring collaboration between technical and non-technical stakeholders.

Video Resources
https://www.youtube.com/watch?v=nS_MRqAeEbQ

Use of ICT

1. Rapid Business Network Modeling

Hyperledger Composer utilizes ICT tools such as JavaScript, Node.js, and npm to model business networks quickly. Developers can define assets, participants, and transaction logic using a domain-specific modeling language, enabling faster creation of blockchain solutions.

2. Integration with Existing Systems

Composer leverages ICT frameworks like LoopBack to integrate blockchain networks with enterprise systems. The REST Server automatically generates APIs for interaction, allowing seamless connectivity between blockchain logic and web or mobile applications.

3. Development Tools

ICT tools such as Visual Studio Code plugins, Yeoman code generators, and the Composer Playground provide developers with user-friendly interfaces for testing and deploying business networks. These tools streamline development processes and enable functional testing without extensive installations.

4. Continuous Integration

Composer supports continuous integration pipelines using tools like GitLab CI. Developers can automate testing, building, and deployment of business network archives (BNAs) to ensure consistent updates to the blockchain environment.

5. Simplified Front-End Integration

Composer's ability to generate Angular applications and REST APIs makes it easier to create front-end interfaces for blockchain networks. This ensures that end users can interact with the network through intuitive web-based applications.

Despite its capabilities, Hyperledger Composer has been deprecated since 2019, and developers are encouraged to use Hyperledger Fabric directly for modern blockchain solutions.

Applications (Real Life/Industrial)

Hyperledger Composer has been widely used to model and deploy blockchain solutions across various industries.

1. Supply Chain Management

- **Use Case**: A "Perishable Goods Network" was built using Hyperledger Composer to track the movement of fruits and vegetables across the supply chain. Participants like farmers, shippers, and importers were assigned specific roles, enabling real-time monitoring of goods, shipment tracking, and payment processing.
- **Impact**: Improved transparency, reduced delays, and ensured the quality of perishable goods during transit.

2. Commodity Trading

- **Use Case**: Hyperledger Composer was used to create a private blockchain network for commodity trading. Assets like commodities were modeled, participants were defined, and transactions were executed securely.
- **Impact**: Enhanced trust among traders, streamlined transaction processes, and reduced fraud risks.

3. Healthcare Data Management

- **Use Case**: Composer facilitated secure sharing of patient data between healthcare providers while maintaining privacy. Patients could control access to their medical records via smart contracts.

- **Impact**: Improved data security, compliance with regulations (like HIPAA), and better coordination among healthcare entities.

4. Financial Services

- **Use Case**: Banks used Composer to create blockchain networks for loan approvals and digital identity verification. Smart contracts automated the approval process based on predefined criteria.
- **Impact**: Faster loan processing times, reduced paperwork, and enhanced customer experience.

5. Education Credentials

- **Use Case**: Universities implemented Composer-based networks to issue blockchain-backed digital certificates for students. These certificates were immutable and easily verifiable by employers.
- **Impact**: Eliminated fake credentials, simplified verification processes, and built trust in academic achievements.

6. Real Estate Transactions

- **Use Case**: Composer was utilized to manage real estate transactions by modeling assets (properties) and participants (buyers/sellers). Smart contracts ensured secure payments and automated title transfers.
- **Impact**: Increased transparency in property deals and reduced legal disputes.

7. Prototype Development for Enterprises

- Hyperledger Composer's Playground allowed businesses to prototype blockchain solutions quickly without needing a full-scale production environment. This was particularly useful for testing use cases before committing resources.

Case-Study (Environmental/Sustainability / Social/Ethical Issues)

Hyperledger Composer for Real Estate Transactions

A real estate company used Hyperledger Composer to streamline its property management and transaction processes. By modeling the business network, they defined **assets** (properties and listings), **participants** (buyers, sellers, and realtors), and **transactions** (creating listings, making offers, and transferring ownership). The blockchain-based system ensured transparency by allowing buyers to view verified property details and track the transaction history securely. Smart contracts automated key processes like payment verification and title transfer, reducing delays and eliminating manual paperwork. The company also integrated the blockchain network with its existing inventory system to update property listings in real-time. This solution enhanced trust among stakeholders, minimized fraud risks, and significantly improved operational efficiency.

Create Inquisitiveness and Curiosity

Imagine a world where blockchain technology simplifies complex business processes like supply chain management, real estate transactions, or healthcare data sharing. How can Hyperledger Composer, with its intuitive modeling tools, help businesses rapidly prototype and deploy blockchain solutions? What if you could create a transparent and tamper-proof system for tracking shipments or verifying academic credentials? How might Composer's integration with existing systems streamline operations and reduce costs? By exploring these questions, you'll uncover the potential of Composer to transform industries and unlock new efficiencies. Dive into case studies where companies have successfully implemented Composer to automate transactions, enhance security, and build trust among stakeholders. This journey of discovery will reveal the exciting possibilities of blockchain technology in real-world applications.

Solved Problems (With increasing difficulty level)

1. Basic: Setting Up a Business Network

Problem: How to create a simple business network using Hyperledger Composer?

Solution:

1. Use Yeoman generator to scaffold a new Composer project
2. Define assets, participants, and transactions in model files
3. Implement transaction logic in JavaScript
4. Deploy the business network to a Hyperledger Fabric runtime

2. Intermediate: Implementing Access Control

Problem: How to restrict access to certain transactions based on participant roles?

Solution:

1. Define participant types (e.g., Buyer, Seller, Regulator)
2. Create an access control language (ACL) file
3. Specify rules that allow or deny access to transactions based on participant type
4. Test access control by attempting transactions with different participant identities

3. Advanced: Integrating with External Systems

Problem: How to integrate a Composer business network with existing enterprise systems?

Solution:

1. Use Composer REST Server to generate APIs for the business network
2. Implement a LoopBack connector to interface with legacy systems
3. Create Node.js applications that use both the Composer API and external system APIs
4. Ensure data consistency between blockchain and external systems through careful transaction design

4. Expert: Optimizing Performance for Large-Scale Deployments

Problem: How to scale a Composer application to handle high transaction volumes?

Solution:

1. Analyze transaction patterns and optimize chaincode
2. Implement caching strategies for frequently accessed data
3. Use private data collections for sensitive information to reduce network load

4. Configure Hyperledger Fabric network for optimal performance (e.g., block size, endorsement policies)
5. Implement off-chain storage solutions for large datasets, keeping only hashes on the blockchain

SUMMARY

- Hyperledger Fabric is a modular and permissioned blockchain framework designed for enterprise solutions.
- The consensus process in Hyperledger Fabric involves endorsement, ordering, and validation phases.
- Key components of Hyperledger Fabric include the distributed ledger, peers, chaincode, MSP, and ordering service.
- Chaincode encapsulates the business logic that governs interactions with the ledger and can be written in multiple languages.
- Advanced functionalities beyond chaincode include Fabric Private Chaincode, chaincode as an external service, and decentralized governance.

EXERCISES

A. Subjective Questions

Category-I ***(Revised Bloom's Level-1, 2 & 3)***

- What are the key features of Hyperledger Fabric that make it suitable for enterprise use?
- Explain the role of each component in the Hyperledger Fabric architecture.
- Describe the steps involved in the consensus process in Hyperledger Fabric.

Category-II ***(Revised Bloom's Level-4, 5 & 6)***

- Compare and contrast the different consensus algorithms available in Hyperledger Fabric.
- Analyze the security implications of using Fabric Private Chaincode.
- Design a Hyperledger Fabric solution for a specific industry use case, such as supply chain management or healthcare.

B. Objective Questions

Category-I ***(Revised Bloom's Level-1, 2 & 3)***

- Which of the following is a key component of Hyperledger Fabric?
  (a) Bitcoin Mining (b) Chaincode
  (c) Proof-of-Stake (d) Ethereum Virtual Machine
- What is the role of the Membership Service Provider (MSP) in Hyperledger Fabric?
- What is the purpose of the ordering service in Hyperledger Fabric?

Category-II ***(Revised Bloom's Level-4, 5 & 6)***

- Which consensus algorithm is best suited for a development environment with a single node?
  (a) Kafka (b) Raft
  (c) Solo (d) PBFT
- How does the optimistic locking model in Hyperledger Fabric handle concurrent transactions?
- What are the benefits of using Fabric Private Chaincode (FPC)?

TEACHER'S KNOW MORE

- Explore the Hyperledger Fabric documentation and tutorials for in-depth information on each topic.
- Research real-world use cases of Hyperledger Fabric in various industries.
- Investigate the latest advancements and features in Hyperledger Fabric, such as decentralized governance and chaincode lifecycle management.

Intentionally Left Blank!

UNIT 4

Use Cases 1 & 2

RATIONALE

This unit explores blockchain's transformative impact on **financial systems** and **supply chains**. Blockchain enhances financial transparency through automated settlements and KYC processes, while in supply chains, it ensures provenance and visibility, optimizing trade finance. By integrating with technologies like IoT and AI, blockchain combats fraud and inefficiencies, offering actionable solutions for businesses and policymakers. This convergence drives operational efficiency, trust, and sustainability, making it a crucial area of study for those seeking to leverage blockchain in reshaping global commerce.

OUTCOMES

- **Understand Blockchain Fundamentals**: Students will grasp the core concepts of blockchain technology, including its architecture, security features, and potential applications in finance and supply chains.
- **Analyze Financial Applications**: Students will learn how blockchain can streamline financial processes such as settlements, KYC/AML compliance, and capital markets through tokenization and smart contracts.
- **Examine Supply Chain Innovations**: Students will explore how blockchain enhances supply chain management by ensuring provenance, improving visibility, and optimizing trade finance through secure invoice management and discounting.
- **Evaluate Real-World Implementations**: Students will analyze case studies and real-world examples to understand the practical challenges and benefits of integrating blockchain into financial and supply chain systems.

4.1 USE CASE 1: BLOCKCHAIN IN FINANCIAL SOFTWARE AND SYSTEMS (FSS): SETTLEMENTS, KYC, CAPITAL MARKETS, INSURANCE

Blockchain technology is revolutionizing the financial sector by addressing inefficiencies, enhancing transparency, and improving security in key areas such as settlements, KYC, capital markets, and insurance. In **settlements**, blockchain eliminates intermediaries by enabling peer-to-peer transactions on a decentralized ledger, significantly reducing processing times and costs. For instance, cross-border payments that traditionally take days can now be settled within seconds using blockchain systems like Ripple or Stellar. This not only enhances efficiency but also ensures transparency and immutability in transaction records, reducing the risk of fraud.

In **KYC (Know Your Customer)** processes as in figure 4.1, blockchain streamlines identity verification and compliance by creating a shared, immutable registry of customer data. Financial institutions can access verified information in real time without duplicating efforts, saving costs and improving accuracy. Platforms like ConsenSys have demonstrated how blockchain can automate KYC/AML (Anti-Money Laundering) processes, ensuring regulatory compliance while enhancing customer onboarding experiences. This reduces operational risks and fosters trust between institutions and their clients.

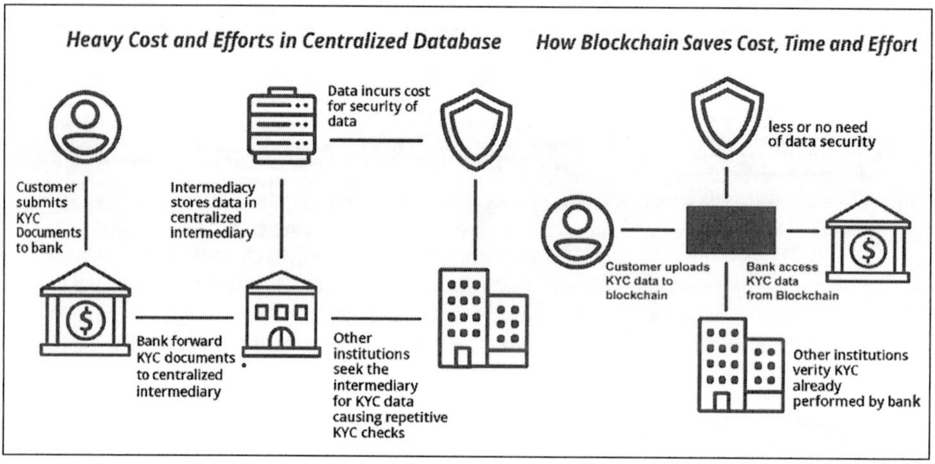

Figure 4.1: *KYC*

For **capital markets**, blockchain facilitates the tokenization of assets, allowing for fractional ownership and faster issuance of digital securities. This innovation expands access to investment opportunities while reducing costs for issuers and investors alike. Smart contracts further automate trading, clearing, and settlement processes, ensuring that transactions are executed efficiently and securely. The use of blockchain in capital markets has also reduced counterparty risks by providing a transparent and tamper-proof record of ownership and transactions.

In the **insurance sector**, blockchain enables automation through smart contracts for claims processing and payouts. Parametric insurance solutions use predefined conditions (e.g., weather data for crop insurance) to trigger instant payouts without manual intervention. Additionally, blockchain enhances fraud detection by maintaining a transparent history of claims across insurers. By integrating blockchain into their operations, insurers can improve customer trust, reduce administrative costs, and ensure faster resolution of claims. These advancements demonstrate how blockchain is transforming financial systems by fostering efficiency, security, and innovation across industries.

4.1.1 Key Benefits of Using Blockchain in Lending Platforms

- **Enhanced Security and Transparency**: Blockchain provides a decentralized and immutable ledger that securely stores transaction records, reducing the risk of data manipulation and fraud. This transparency also helps in maintaining regulatory compliance and building trust among stakeholders.
- **Streamlined Processes and Efficiency**: Blockchain automates loan processing through smart contracts, which execute transactions based on predefined conditions. This reduces manual verification processes, speeds up loan approvals, and minimizes administrative costs.

- **Improved Credit Scoring and Risk Assessment**: Blockchain can aggregate credit data across networks, enabling more accurate credit scoring and risk assessment. This helps lenders make informed decisions while reducing the risk of default.
- **Increased Financial Inclusion**: By reducing intermediaries and transaction costs, blockchain-based lending platforms can offer more accessible financial services to underserved populations, enhancing financial inclusion.

Video Resources
https://www.youtube.com/watch?v=WhjqfjBrDLg

Use of ICT

Information and Communication Technology (ICT) is integral to the implementation of blockchain in financial systems like settlements, KYC, capital markets, and insurance. ICT enables the seamless integration of blockchain networks with existing financial infrastructure, facilitating real-time transaction processing and data sharing. Through distributed ledger technology (DLT), ICT ensures secure and transparent operations, eliminating intermediaries and reducing costs. Smart contracts automate workflows, streamlining processes such as claims management in insurance or asset tokenization in capital markets. Additionally, ICT supports compliance by enabling automated audit trails and regulatory reporting. This combination enhances efficiency, security, and scalability across financial services.

Applications (Real Life/Industrial)

- **Cross-Border Payments and Settlements**: Blockchain networks, such as Ripple and Stellar, enable instant cross-border transactions by eliminating intermediaries like correspondent banks. This reduces transaction fees and settlement times from days to seconds, making international payments more efficient and accessible. For example, blockchain has been used to streamline remittance services for migrant workers, offering low-cost and real-time payment solutions.
- **Crypto-Collateralized Lending**: Blockchain-based lending platforms allow loans to be collateralized using crypto assets like Bitcoin. These platforms provide transparency, as the value of collateral can be verified in real-time through market prices. Additionally, smart contracts automate loan agreements, reducing risks and operational costs for lenders. Platforms like Aave and Compound are leading examples of decentralized lending systems leveraging blockchain.
- **Clearing and Settlement Systems**: Blockchain technology modernizes clearing and settlement processes in financial markets by automating transactions with smart contracts. This reduces counterparty risk, eliminates intermediaries, and ensures swift transaction finality. For instance, the Bank of England explored blockchain-based gross settlement systems to enhance resilience and transparency in payment processing.

Case-Study (Environmental/Sustainability/Social/Ethical Issues)

Blockchain technology has demonstrated its potential to address environmental and sustainability challenges, particularly in supply chain transparency and carbon emissions tracking. For instance, IBM's blockchain-based platform, Provenance, has been used to verify the ethical sourcing of goods and ensure environmentally sustainable practices in industries such as forestry and agriculture. By creating tamper-proof records of product origins and production methods, blockchain helps combat illegal logging and promotes sustainable resource management. Additionally, blockchain enables efficient tracking of carbon credits, ensuring that emissions reductions are accurately recorded and not fraudulently claimed. While energy consumption remains a concern, advancements like Ethereum's shift to the energy-efficient Proof-of-Stake consensus mechanism have reduced environmental impacts by up to 99.95%, showcasing blockchain's adaptability in supporting sustainability goals.

Create Inquisitiveness and Curiosity

Imagine a financial world where transactions are lightning-fast, secure, and transparent, thanks to blockchain technology. How can blockchain transform traditional financial systems by automating settlements, enhancing KYC processes, and tokenizing assets in capital markets? What if blockchain could revolutionize insurance by automating claims processing and ensuring fraud-proof records? As you delve into these questions, you'll uncover the exciting possibilities of blockchain in reshaping global finance. Explore how companies like JPMorgan and HSBC are leveraging blockchain to streamline cross-border payments and compliance. Dive into case studies where blockchain has improved operational efficiency, reduced costs, and enhanced customer trust. This journey of discovery will reveal the transformative power of blockchain in real-world financial applications, sparking curiosity about its potential to redefine the future of finance.

Solved Problems (With Increasing Difficulty Level)

1. Basic: Faster Cross-Border Payments

- **Problem**: Traditional cross-border payments are slow, expensive, and involve multiple intermediaries, leading to delays and high transaction fees.
- **Solution**: Blockchain-based payment platforms like Ripple and Stellar enable near-instant settlements by eliminating intermediaries. Transactions are processed directly between parties on a decentralized ledger, reducing costs and settlement times from days to seconds. This has transformed remittance services, making them more affordable and efficient for users worldwide.

2. Intermediate: Streamlining KYC/AML Compliance

- **Problem**: Banks face redundant processes in Know Your Customer (KYC) and Anti-Money Laundering (AML) compliance, leading to inefficiencies, high costs, and data silos.
- **Solution**: Blockchain creates a shared, immutable registry of customer data accessible to authorized institutions. Platforms like ConsenSys automate KYC/AML processes, enabling real-time verification while reducing duplication and operational risks. This ensures compliance, speeds up onboarding, and saves costs for financial institutions.

3. Advanced: Tokenization of Assets in Capital Markets

- **Problem**: Traditional capital markets suffer from inefficiencies in asset issuance, trading, and settlement due to manual processes and lack of transparency.

- **Solution**: Blockchain facilitates the tokenization of assets such as stocks or real estate into digital tokens that can be traded on decentralized platforms. This increases liquidity, enables fractional ownership, and reduces settlement times from days to seconds. For example, JPMorgan's Onyx platform uses blockchain for tokenized securities trading, ensuring secure and efficient transactions while reducing counterparty risks.

4.2 USE CASE 2: BLOCKCHAIN IN TRADE/SUPPLY CHAIN: PROVENANCE OF GOODS, VISIBILITY, TRADE/SUPPLY CHAIN FINANCE, INVOICE MANAGEMENT DISCOUNTING, ETC

Blockchain technology is transforming trade and supply chain management by addressing critical challenges such as provenance, visibility, and efficiency. Provenance tracking ensures authenticity by recording the origin and journey of goods on an immutable ledger. For example, De Beers uses blockchain to trace diamonds from mines to retailers, preventing conflict diamonds from entering the market. This level of transparency builds trust among consumers and stakeholders, ensuring ethical sourcing and compliance with industry standards.

Visibility in supply chains is enhanced through real-time tracking powered by blockchain integrated with IoT devices like RFID tags and smart sensors. These tools monitor conditions such as temperature and humidity throughout the logistics process, ensuring product integrity during transit. Blockchain also creates secure audit trails for logistics synchronization, reducing administrative overheads and enabling automated settlements. Companies like IBM Food Trust have implemented blockchain to improve food safety by tracing products from farm to table, minimizing contamination risks.

Trade finance and invoice management benefit significantly from blockchain's automation capabilities. Smart contracts streamline workflows by automatically triggering payments or approvals when predefined conditions are met. This reduces bottlenecks, clerical errors, and fraud risks while improving cash flow for businesses. Blockchain-based platforms also facilitate invoice discounting by providing verified transaction records to financial institutions, enabling faster access to working capital for suppliers.

By integrating blockchain into supply chain systems, businesses achieve higher efficiency and resilience against disruptions. Blockchain's decentralized infrastructure provides a shared version of truth across all participants, fostering collaboration while reducing disputes. As the blockchain supply chain market grows at a projected CAGR of 29.14%, reaching $9.77 billion by 2030, its adoption is set to redefine global trade practices with sustainable and transparent solutions.

4.2.1 How Does Blockchain Improve the Visibility of Goods in the Supply Chain

Blockchain improves the visibility of goods in the supply chain by creating a transparent and immutable record of transactions, enabling real-time tracking and traceability. By integrating blockchain with technologies like IoT sensors and RFID tags, companies can monitor the location, condition (e.g., temperature, humidity), and movement of goods at every stage of the supply chain. This data is securely stored on a decentralized ledger, accessible to all authorized stakeholders, ensuring a single source of truth for logistics synchronization and compliance management.

Blockchain also enhances traceability by recording detailed information about goods, such as origin, quality certifications, and production processes. This helps businesses combat counterfeiting, reduce losses from gray market trading, and ensure ethical sourcing. For example, companies in industries like pharmaceuticals and luxury goods use blockchain to verify product authenticity and prevent fraud. Additionally, blockchain's ability to digitize physical assets allows for seamless tracking from production to delivery or end-user consumption.

The technology also facilitates better collaboration among supply chain participants by providing shared access to real-time data. This reduces communication errors, minimizes delays, and streamlines administrative tasks like audits and compliance checks. Smart contracts further automate workflows by triggering actions such as payment releases or inventory updates when predefined conditions are met.

Overall, blockchain's integration into supply chains not only improves operational efficiency but also builds trust among stakeholders. By offering enhanced visibility and transparency, blockchain ensures that businesses can proactively address risks like counterfeit goods or regulatory violations while enhancing their reputation for responsible manufacturing.

4.2.2 Benefits of Using Blockchain for Invoice Management and Discounting

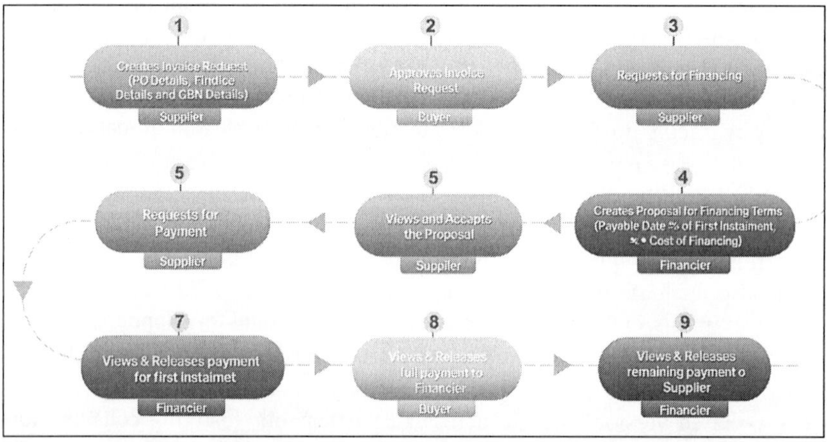

Figure 4.2: *Invoice Discounting Process*

The main benefits of using blockchain for invoice management and discounting include

- **Enhanced Transparency and Trust**: Blockchain provides a decentralized, immutable ledger that serves as a single source of truth for all transactions. This ensures that all parties involved in the invoice discounting process have real-time access to verified information, reducing disputes and fraud risks.
- **Automation and Efficiency**: Blockchain automates the invoice discounting process by using smart contracts to trigger payments and settlements in real-time. This eliminates manual steps, streamlines documentation, and accelerates cash flow for suppliers.
- **Improved Risk Management**: Blockchain's transparent and tamper-proof records allow for better risk profiling of clients. By analyzing transaction histories stored on

the blockchain, financial institutions can assess creditworthiness more accurately, reducing the risk of non-payment.

- **Increased Security and Compliance**: Blockchain technology ensures the confidentiality and integrity of data exchanged during invoice discounting. It also provides a legal framework for transactions, preventing double invoicing and ensuring that all assignments are recorded immutably.

Video Resources
https://www.youtube.com/watch?v=u7NWVUVujEQ

Use of ICT

ICT plays a pivotal role in enabling blockchain solutions for financial systems and supply chains. In **financial software**, technologies like cloud computing, IoT, and distributed ledger systems facilitate secure settlements, streamlined KYC processes, and tokenized capital markets, enhancing transparency and reducing operational inefficiencies1. Similarly, in **trade and supply chains**, ICT integrates blockchain with IoT sensors and AI to ensure provenance of goods, improve visibility across networks, automate invoice management, and enable smart contracts for supply chain finance. These applications foster trust among stakeholders while addressing challenges like data authenticity, compliance, and scalability.

Applications (Real Life/Industrial)

- **Settlements and Payments**: Blockchain enables instant and cost-effective cross-border payments by eliminating intermediaries and automating processes through smart contracts, reducing settlement times from days to seconds.
- **KYC/AML Compliance**: Blockchain streamlines Know Your Customer (KYC) and Anti-Money Laundering (AML) processes by creating shared, immutable registries for customer data, ensuring real-time verification and reducing duplication across institutions.
- **Capital Markets and Asset Tokenization**: Blockchain facilitates the tokenization of assets, enabling fractional ownership, faster issuance of digital securities, and enhanced liquidity in capital markets.

Case-Study (Environmental/Sustainability/Social/Ethical Issues)

Shinhan Bank in South Korea leveraged blockchain technology to innovate its foreign currency remittance system. Collaborating with Streami, a blockchain startup, the bank developed a secure and efficient platform that eliminated reliance on traditional intermediaries like SWIFT. Through blockchain's decentralized ledger, transactions were processed faster, reducing costs and enhancing transparency. Additionally, Shinhan introduced Digital Kiosk services, which utilized blockchain for palm vein recognition and secure data storage, ensuring customer authentication without reuse risks. These initiatives streamlined financial processes, reduced operational costs, and set a precedent for integrating blockchain into banking systems for improved efficiency and security.

Create Inquisitiveness and Curiosity

Imagine a world where financial transactions are instant, secure, and transparent, eliminating intermediaries and reducing costs. How can blockchain transform industries like banking, insurance, and capital markets by automating settlements, enhancing KYC processes, and tokenizing assets? In supply chains, picture a scenario where goods are tracked from origin to consumer, ensuring authenticity and visibility across networks. What if blockchain could optimize trade finance, automate invoice management, and enable smart contracts for seamless transactions?

By exploring these questions, you'll uncover the exciting possibilities of blockchain in reshaping global commerce and fostering trust among stakeholders. Dive into case studies where companies have successfully implemented blockchain solutions to streamline operations, reduce fraud risks, and enhance customer experience. This journey of discovery will reveal the transformative power of blockchain in real-world applications.

Solved Problems (With Increasing Difficulty Level)

1. Basic: Streamlining Cross-Border Payments

- **Problem**: Traditional cross-border payments are slow, expensive, and involve multiple intermediaries, leading to high transaction fees and delays.
- **Solution**: Blockchain eliminates intermediaries by using a decentralized ledger to process payments directly between parties. For example, Ripple's blockchain-based payment system enables near-instant settlements with fees reduced by up to 80%. This ensures faster, cheaper, and more secure transactions compared to traditional banking systems.

2. Intermediate: Enhancing KYC/AML Compliance

- **Problem**: Banks face challenges in managing Know Your Customer (KYC) and Anti-Money Laundering (AML) compliance due to redundant processes and lack of centralized data sharing.
- **Solution**: Blockchain enables shared KYC/AML registries where customer data is securely stored and accessed by authorized institutions. This reduces duplication, speeds up onboarding, and ensures compliance. For instance, HSBC implemented a blockchain-based KYC platform that reduced verification time by 40% while improving data accuracy.

3. Advanced: Tokenization of Assets in Capital Markets

- **Problem**: Traditional capital markets struggle with inefficiencies in asset issuance, trading, and settlement due to manual processes and lack of transparency.
- **Solution**: Blockchain facilitates the tokenization of assets like stocks, bonds, or real estate into digital tokens that can be traded on decentralized platforms. This increases liquidity, enables fractional ownership, and reduces settlement times from days to seconds. JPMorgan's Onyx platform is an example of blockchain being used for tokenized securities trading and instant settlements.

SUMMARY

- **Enhances Settlements**: Blockchain streamlines cross-border payments by reducing transaction times and costs.
- **Streamlines KYC/AML**: Blockchain automates compliance processes through shared customer data registries.

- **Tokenizes Assets**: Blockchain enables fractional ownership and faster issuance of digital securities.
- **Automates Insurance Claims**: Blockchain uses smart contracts for faster and fraud-proof claims processing.
- **Ensures Provenance**: Blockchain tracks goods' origin and journey to combat counterfeiting.
- **Improves Visibility**: Blockchain integrates with IoT for real-time tracking across supply chains.
- **Streamlines Trade Finance**: Blockchain automates workflows and reduces paperwork in trade finance.
- **Automates Invoice Management**: Blockchain prevents double financing and fraud through tamper-proof ledgers.
- **Enhances Security**: Blockchain ensures secure and tamper-proof transaction records.
- **Fosters Transparency and Trust**: Blockchain provides a transparent and immutable ledger for all stakeholders.

EXERCISES

A. Subjective Questions

Category-I *(Revised Bloom's Levels-1, 2 & 3: Remember, Understand, Apply)*

- Define blockchain and explain its role in financial software systems like settlements and KYC.
- Describe how blockchain ensures transparency and traceability in supply chain management.
- Explain the process of asset tokenization in capital markets using blockchain technology.

Category-II *(Revised Bloom's Levels-4, 5 & 6: Analyze, Evaluate, Create)*

- Analyze the impact of blockchain on reducing fraud in insurance claims processing.
- Evaluate the advantages and challenges of using blockchain for invoice management and discounting.
- Propose a blockchain-based solution to enhance trade finance efficiency in global supply chains.

B. Objective Questions

Category-I *(Revised Bloom's Levels-1, 2 & 3: Remember, Understand, Apply)*

1. What is the primary benefit of using blockchain for cross-border settlements?

   (a) Increased transaction speed

   (b) Higher transaction costs

   (c) Reduced transparency

   (d) Dependence on intermediaries

2. Which technology is often integrated with blockchain to improve supply chain visibility?

   (a) IoT sensors (b) Cloud computing

   (c) Big data analytics (d) Artificial intelligence

3. Blockchain facilitates KYC by:

   (a) Storing customer data on centralized servers

   (b) Creating a shared, immutable registry for real-time verification

   (c) Eliminating the need for compliance checks

   (d) Increasing manual processes

Category-II ***(Revised Bloom's Levels-4, 5 & 6: Analyze, Evaluate, Create)***

- Analyze how smart contracts can automate workflows in trade finance and reduce risks.
- Evaluate the environmental and ethical concerns associated with blockchain adoption in financial systems.
- Design a blockchain-based framework to enhance transparency in tracking the provenance of goods in supply chains.

TEACHER'S KNOW MORE

- Blockchain enhances financial systems by streamlining settlements, automating KYC/AML, and facilitating asset tokenization.
- Blockchain ensures provenance and visibility in supply chains, combating counterfeiting and promoting ethical sourcing.
- Blockchain improves operational efficiency and security across industries by automating workflows and providing tamper-proof records.

UNIT 5

Use Case 3

RATIONALE

This chapter explores the transformative potential of blockchain technology in government operations, focusing on key areas such as digital identity management, land records, and other forms of record-keeping. Blockchain enables secure and tamper-proof digital identities, reducing identity fraud and enhancing trust between citizens and governments. It also provides an immutable ledger for land records, minimizing disputes over ownership and reducing corruption in land registries. Furthermore, blockchain can streamline public distribution systems (PDS) and social welfare by ensuring that subsidies or benefits reach the intended recipients without intermediaries, thereby enhancing accountability and efficiency. Additionally, the chapter delves into blockchain cryptography, highlighting how techniques like hashing and digital signatures secure data, and addresses privacy and security concerns through methods such as zero-knowledge proofs and permissioned blockchains. By examining these applications and challenges, the chapter provides a comprehensive understanding of blockchain's potential to revolutionize government functions by fostering transparency, security, and citizen trust.

OUTCOMES

- Understand blockchain's role in secure digital identities and record-keeping.
- Explore blockchain's efficiency in public distribution and welfare systems.
- Learn cryptographic techniques securing blockchain transactions.
- Examine privacy and security measures in blockchain applications.

5.1 BLOCKCHAIN FOR GOVERNMENT:DIGITAL IDENTITY, LAND RECORDS AND OTHER KINDS OF RECORD KEEPING BETWEEN GOVERNMENT ENTITIES

Blockchain technology is revolutionizing government operations by providing secure, transparent, and efficient solutions for record-keeping and digital identity management. Traditional centralized systems often suffer from inefficiencies, high costs, and vulnerabilities to corruption or data breaches. Blockchain's decentralized nature eliminates single points of failure, ensuring tamper-proof and traceable records. For digital identity, blockchain enables secure identity verification through distributed ledger technology (DLT), reducing risks of identity theft and enhancing privacy. Governments can use blockchain to create e-identities that streamline access to public services while safeguarding sensitive citizen data.

Land record management as given in figure 5.1 is another area where blockchain offers transformative potential. Centralized land registries are prone to fraud, mismanagement, and data loss due to natural disasters or cyberattacks. Blockchain-based land registry systems ensure transparency by maintaining immutable records of property ownership and transactions. These systems allow for real-time updates, reduce disputes over ownership, and eliminate the need for intermediaries. For example, countries like Sweden have tested blockchain for land registration to enhance efficiency and trust in property transactions.

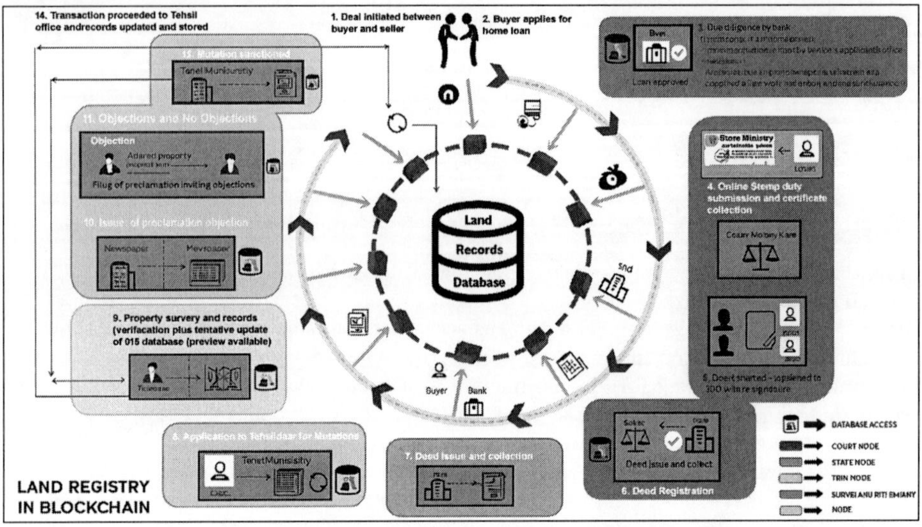

***Figure 5.1:** Land records in Blockchain*

Beyond digital identity and land records, blockchain can streamline various government functions such as public procurement, benefits disbursement, and inter-agency coordination. Smart contracts on blockchain automate processes by executing predefined conditions without manual intervention, reducing bureaucracy and corruption. Governments worldwide are exploring blockchain's potential in building smart cities, managing public healthcare, and even conducting secure electronic voting. By fostering transparency and accountability, blockchain not only enhances operational efficiency but also strengthens public trust in government institutions.

5.1.1 Challenges in implementing blockchain-based land record systems

Implementing blockchain-based land record systems presents several challenges that must be addressed for successful adoption. One of the primary issues is the **digitization of existing records**. Many countries, especially in the developing world, still rely on paper-based cadastres that are incomplete or outdated. Blockchain systems require accurate and digital data because once information is recorded on a blockchain, it becomes immutable. Errors, fraud, or corruption in the initial data could perpetuate inaccuracies indefinitely. The process of digitizing and verifying these records is resource-intensive and requires significant investment in infrastructure and expertise.

Another critical challenge is **integration with existing legal and administrative frameworks**. Blockchain-based systems must comply with local land ownership laws and regulations, which vary widely across jurisdictions. This necessitates collaboration between technical experts, legal professionals, and government authorities to ensure seamless integration without disrupting current processes. Additionally, establishing legal recognition of blockchain-based land records may require amendments to existing laws or the creation of new frameworks to accommodate the unique characteristics of blockchain technology.

Finally, **scalability and adoption issues** pose significant hurdles. Land registry systems must handle large volumes of transactions and data, making scalability a crucial consideration. Blockchain technology, while offering transparency and security, faces performance limitations when processing high transaction volumes. Furthermore, public awareness and trust in blockchain technology are essential for widespread adoption. Governments must invest in educating stakeholders about its benefits while addressing concerns about data privacy, governance, and the potential misuse of technology by corrupt officials or malicious actors.

Use of ICT

The integration of blockchain technology into government operations relies heavily on Information and Communication Technology (ICT) infrastructure to ensure seamless implementation and functionality. ICT systems enable the creation and management of secure digital identities by leveraging blockchain's decentralized and tamper-proof architecture, allowing governments to issue e-identities stored on blockchain for secure access to public services. For land records, ICT infrastructure is crucial for digitizing existing records and integrating them into a distributed ledger, ensuring property ownership data is immutable and transparent. Additionally, ICT tools like Geographic Information Systems (GIS) can be integrated with blockchain to provide spatial data for land management. Beyond these applications, ICT facilitates the management of diverse government records such as birth certificates and business licenses through blockchain, enabling interoperability between agencies while maintaining data security and transparency. Smart contracts, supported by ICT infrastructure, automate processes like public procurement and benefits disbursement, reducing bureaucracy and corruption. Overall, ICT serves as the backbone for implementing blockchain in government functions by providing the necessary digital tools for data storage, processing, and integration across various sectors.

Applications (Real Life/Industrial)

- **Digital Identity: Estonia's e-Residency Program** Estonia's e-Residency program is a pioneering example of blockchain-based digital identity. Launched in 2014, it allows individuals worldwide to establish a digital identity and access services like banking and business registration in Estonia. The system uses blockchain technology to secure identity data, ensuring that only authorized users can access or share information, thereby enhancing security and reducing bureaucracy.
- **Land Records: Sweden's Blockchain Land Registry** Sweden has experimented with blockchain technology for land registry management. This initiative aims to enhance transparency and efficiency in property transactions by maintaining immutable records of ownership and transactions. It reduces disputes over ownership and eliminates the need for intermediaries, making the process more secure and streamlined.
- **Other Record Keeping: Blockchain-Based Public Procurement in Dubai** Dubai has explored the use of blockchain for public procurement processes. By posting and administering government contracts on a distributed ledger, Dubai ensures transparency and accountability while maintaining confidentiality where necessary. This approach reduces fraud and corruption, making procurement processes more efficient and trustworthy.

Case-Study (Environmental/Sustainability/Social/Ethical Issues)

A notable case study of blockchain implementation in government is the **Zug Digital ID project** in Switzerland, which introduced self-sovereign identities using the Ethereum blockchain. Launched as a pilot in 2017, this initiative allowed residents of Zug to register their digital IDs on a public blockchain through the uPort platform. The system enabled citizens to securely manage their identities, verify credentials, and participate in e-voting without intermediaries. For example, during a local referendum, 70 citizens voted on festival fireworks using their blockchain-based IDs, demonstrating the potential for secure, transparent, and efficient digital interactions between governments and citizens. This project showcased how blockchain could modernize public services while empowering individuals to control their personal data and reducing administrative costs for governments.

Create Inquisitiveness and Curiosity

Imagine a world where your identity is secure and portable, where land ownership is transparent and tamper-proof, and where government records are accessible yet protected from corruption. Blockchain technology is transforming the way governments manage digital identities, land records, and other critical data by offering a decentralized, immutable ledger that ensures transparency and accountability. But how exactly does this work? How can blockchain prevent identity theft while allowing seamless access to public services? What if land disputes could be resolved instantly with blockchain-based property records? And what potential does this hold for revolutionizing public procurement, healthcare, and even voting systems? As governments begin to adopt blockchain solutions, the possibilities are vast and intriguing—raising questions about what the future of governance might look like with this technology at its core.

Solved Problems (With increasing difficulty level)

Simplifying Business Registrations in British Columbia (Easy)

The Canadian province of British Columbia implemented the OrgBook BC project, a blockchain-based decentralized identity system for small businesses. This platform provides a searchable directory of verifiable public data about over 525,000 legal entities, such as business licenses and permits, issued by government authorities. By leveraging blockchain, the project simplifies access to business credentials and eliminates inefficiencies in verifying government-issued documents.

Secure Digital Identity in Zug, Switzerland (Moderate)

The city of Zug launched a pilot project using Ethereum blockchain to create self-sovereign digital identities for its residents. Citizens could register their digital IDs, securely manage their data, and participate in e-voting without intermediaries. For instance, 70 residents used their blockchain-based IDs to vote on local issues like festival fireworks, demonstrating how blockchain can modernize governance while ensuring security and transparency.

Streamlining Land Transactions in Sweden (Challenging)

Sweden's Chromaway project utilized blockchain to automate property transactions and maintain tamper-proof land records. By integrating smart contracts into real estate processes, the system reduced uncertainties between parties and eliminated intermediaries. However, challenges like ensuring legal recognition of digital signatures had to be addressed to fully operationalize the system, showcasing the complexities of applying blockchain to high-value transactions like real estate.

5.2 PUBLIC DISTRIBUTION SYSTEM SOCIAL WELFARE SYSTEMS BLOCKCHAIN CRYPTOGRAPHY,PRIVACY AND SECURITY ON BLOCKCHAIN

Blockchain technology has emerged as a transformative tool for enhancing the efficiency, transparency, and security of public distribution systems (PDS), social welfare programs, and record-keeping in government entities. In the context of PDS, blockchain can address long-standing issues such as leakage, corruption, and exclusion errors by creating an immutable ledger for tracking food grain supplies from warehouses to beneficiaries. For instance, India's conceptual framework for blockchain-enabled PDS proposes using smart contracts and unique identifiers like QR codes to ensure transparency in transactions and prevent fraud. This system not only reduces wastage and delays but also provides real-time data on stock availability, fostering trust among stakeholders.

Social welfare systems can also benefit significantly from blockchain's cryptographic capabilities to enhance privacy and security. Blockchain ensures that sensitive beneficiary data is encrypted and stored securely, preventing unauthorized access or tampering. Smart contracts automate welfare disbursements based on predefined eligibility criteria, reducing administrative inefficiencies and delays. Dubai's blockchain initiatives in public procurement and welfare payments exemplify how governments can leverage distributed ledger technology to improve accountability while safeguarding citizen data.

Cryptography forms the backbone of blockchain's privacy and security features, enabling governments to protect sensitive records while ensuring transparency. Blockchain's decentralized nature eliminates single points of failure, making it resistant to cyberattacks and data breaches. For applications like land records, governments can use blockchain to maintain tamper-proof property ownership data, reducing disputes and fraud. West Bengal's partnership with Airchains to digitize land ownership records through NFTs on Polygon demonstrates how blockchain can modernize traditional bureaucratic processes while ensuring data integrity. The Blockchain Based Public Distribution is as shown in figure 5.2.

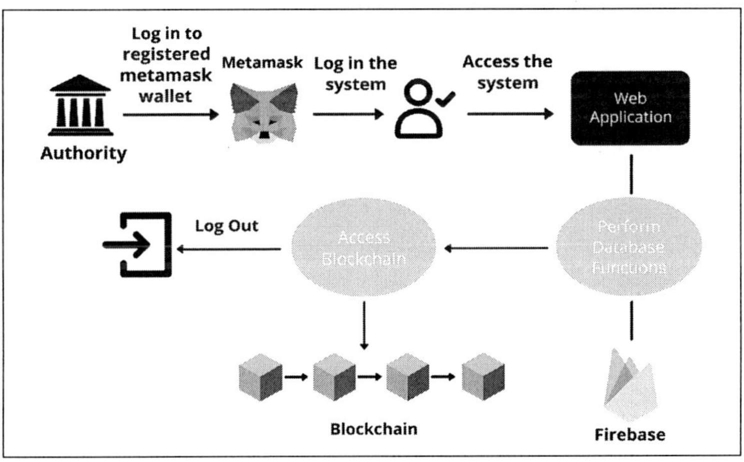

Figure 5.2: *Blockchain Based Public Distribution*

5.2.1 Benefits of Using Blockchain for Public Distribution Systems

- **Enhanced Transparency and Accountability** Blockchain ensures that every transaction in public distribution and welfare systems is recorded on an immutable ledger, making it tamper-proof and easily auditable. This transparency reduces corruption and ensures that resources such as food grains or welfare funds reach the intended beneficiaries without leakages or fraud.
- **Improved Data Privacy and Security** Blockchain uses advanced cryptographic techniques to secure sensitive data, such as citizen identities and transaction details. Its decentralized nature eliminates single points of failure, protecting against data breaches and unauthorized access. This is particularly critical for social welfare systems, where personal information must remain private while still being accessible for legitimate purposes.
- **Efficiency Through Automation** Smart contracts on blockchain automate processes like eligibility verification and fund disbursement in welfare programs or inventory tracking in public distribution systems. This reduces administrative overhead, minimizes errors, and speeds up service delivery. For instance, blockchain can track the movement of food grains in real time, ensuring timely delivery and reducing wastage.

5.2.2 Barriers to Implementing Blockchain in Public Distribution System

- **Technological Challenges**: Blockchain systems face scalability and interoperability issues, particularly when handling large volumes of transactions, as required in PDS. The lack of interoperability between different blockchain networks and legacy systems further complicates integration. Additionally, blockchain's high energy consumption for consensus mechanisms like Proof of Work can be a concern for large-scale adoption in resource-constrained settings.
- **Organizational Barriers**: Resistance to change within government institutions is a significant hurdle. Many stakeholders lack awareness or understanding of blockchain technology, which leads to skepticism about its benefits. Furthermore, the absence of skilled professionals to develop, deploy, and maintain blockchain systems exacerbates the problem. Trust among participants in the blockchain network and concerns over data governance also pose challenges.
- **Financial and Regulatory Constraints**: Implementing blockchain requires substantial upfront investment in infrastructure and training, which can be a deterrent for governments with limited budgets. Additionally, the lack of clear regulatory frameworks for blockchain technology creates uncertainty and risk for its adoption in public systems like PDS. Governments must address these regulatory gaps to ensure compliance and build confidence among stakeholders.

Video Resources
https://www.youtube.com/watch?v=CdK6h_UHufE

Use of ICT

The use of Information and Communication Technology (ICT) in the Public Distribution System (PDS) has significantly enhanced its efficiency, transparency, and accountability.

ICT tools such as Electronic Point of Sale (e-PoS) devices authenticate beneficiaries through Aadhaar or other digital IDs, ensuring that subsidized food grains reach the intended recipients while reducing leakages and fraud. GPS and IoT technologies enable real-time tracking of food grain movement across the supply chain, ensuring proper delivery to fair price shops. Additionally, smart ration cards and blockchain technology provide tamper-proof records of transactions, creating a transparent system that minimizes corruption and inefficiencies. These advancements demonstrate how ICT can revolutionize PDS operations by streamlining processes and improving service delivery to vulnerable populations.

Applications (Real Life/Industrial)

- **Blockchain in Public Distribution Systems (PDS)** Blockchain has been proposed as a solution to prevent leakages and corruption in India's Public Distribution System. By creating an immutable ledger that tracks food grain supplies from warehouses to Fair Price Shops (FPS), blockchain ensures transparency and accountability at every stage. Smart contracts automate the distribution process, while GPS integration provides real-time tracking of supplies, reducing inefficiencies and ensuring that resources reach the intended beneficiaries.
- **Blockchain in Social Welfare Systems** Governments can use blockchain to streamline welfare disbursements by automating processes through smart contracts. For example, Dubai has implemented blockchain for welfare payments, ensuring that funds are distributed only to eligible recipients without delays or intermediaries. This reduces administrative overhead while securing sensitive beneficiary data through cryptographic encryption, enhancing privacy and trust in the system.
- **Cryptography, Privacy, and Security on Blockchain** Blockchain's cryptographic features ensure data privacy and security in government systems by encrypting sensitive information like citizen identities and welfare records. Its decentralized nature eliminates single points of failure, making it resistant to cyberattacks. For instance, private blockchains used in government systems allow role-based access to data, ensuring that only authorized personnel can view or modify records while maintaining transparency for auditing purposes.

Case-Study (Environmental/Sustainability/Social/Ethical Issues)

A case study on the application of blockchain in India's Public Distribution System (PDS) highlights its potential to address long-standing issues such as corruption, leakage, and inefficiencies in the supply chain. The proposed blockchain framework tracks food grains from warehouses to Fair Price Shops (FPS) using an immutable ledger, ensuring transparency and accountability at every stage. By integrating smart contracts, the system automates processes like verifying eligibility and generating payment slips for farmers and millers, reducing delays and administrative overhead. Unique identifiers such as QR codes or RFID tags are used to track grain bags, ensuring accurate data on quantity and quality. This blockchain-enabled system also provides real-time alerts for stock management and prevents wastage due to prolonged storage. By decentralizing data and making it tamper-proof, the system enhances trust among stakeholders while ensuring that subsidized food grains reach the intended beneficiaries efficiently and securely.

Create Inquisitiveness and Curiosity

Imagine a world where government welfare programs are seamless, corruption-free, and fully transparent. Blockchain technology offers the potential to revolutionize public distribution systems and social welfare programs by creating immutable records of transactions, ensuring that subsidies and benefits reach the intended recipients without leakages or fraud. But how does blockchain achieve this? With cryptographic security and decentralized ledgers, blockchain ensures privacy while providing tamper-proof data storage. What if every food grain distributed or welfare payment made could be tracked in real-time, with complete accountability? The possibilities are endless—could blockchain be the key to solving inefficiencies in government systems while safeguarding sensitive citizen data?

Solved Problems (With increasing difficulty level)

Improving Transparency in India's Public Distribution System (PDS)

A conceptual framework for blockchain-enabled PDS in India was proposed to address issues like leakage, corruption, and exclusion errors. By using blockchain to track food grains from warehouses to Fair Price Shops (FPS), the system ensures transparency and accountability. Smart contracts automate processes such as payments to farmers and millers, while QR codes or RFID tags enable real-time tracking of grain supplies. This approach reduces inefficiencies, improves stock management, and ensures that subsidized food grains reach the intended beneficiaries without diversion or fraud.

Streamlining Welfare Payments in Dubai

Dubai implemented blockchain technology in its social welfare systems to enhance efficiency and security. By leveraging smart contracts, welfare disbursements were automated based on predefined eligibility criteria, eliminating delays and reducing administrative overhead. Blockchain's cryptographic features ensured that beneficiary data remained secure while preventing unauthorized access. This system not only improved accountability but also built trust among citizens by ensuring that funds reached the right recipients without intermediaries.

Securing Land Records with Blockchain in West Bengal

In West Bengal, India, the New Town Kolkata Development Authority partnered with Airchains to digitize land ownership records using blockchain technology. By deploying NFTs on Polygon Supernets, the system replaced traditional bureaucratic processes with a transparent and tamper-proof digital ledger. This initiative addressed challenges like property disputes and data tampering while ensuring privacy through cryptographic encryption. The project demonstrated how blockchain could modernize government record-keeping systems while maintaining both security and transparency.

SUMMARY

- **Blockchain for Digital Identity**: Enhances security and reduces identity fraud.
- **Blockchain for Land Records**: Provides an immutable ledger for ownership verification.
- **Blockchain for Record Keeping**: Streamlines inter-governmental data management.

- **Blockchain in Public Distribution Systems (PDS)**: Ensures transparency and reduces leakages.
- **Blockchain in Social Welfare**: Automates benefit disbursement to intended recipients.
- **Blockchain Cryptography**: Utilizes hashing and digital signatures for data integrity.
- **Blockchain Privacy**: Employs zero-knowledge proofs and encryption for data protection.
- **Blockchain Security**: Offers decentralized data storage to mitigate cyber threats.
- **Blockchain Scalability**: Faces challenges in handling high transaction volumes.
- **Blockchain Adoption**: Requires regulatory frameworks for widespread government use.

EXERCISES

A. Subjective Questions

Category-I *(Revised Bloom's Level-1, 2 & 3)*

1. Define blockchain and explain its importance in digital identity management.
2. Describe how blockchain ensures transparency and security in land record management.
3. Explain the role of cryptographic techniques in securing blockchain transactions.
4. Discuss the challenges faced by public distribution systems (PDS) and how blockchain can address them.

Category-II *(Revised Bloom's Level-4, 5 & 6)*

1. Analyze the privacy concerns associated with blockchain's transparency and propose solutions to mitigate them.
2. Evaluate the effectiveness of blockchain in preventing fraud in social welfare systems.
3. Design a framework for implementing blockchain in inter-governmental record-keeping systems.
4. Critically assess the role of zero-knowledge proofs in enhancing privacy on blockchain networks.

B. Objective Questions

Category-I *(Revised Bloom's Level-1, 2 & 3)*

1. What is the primary function of hashing in a blockchain?

   (a) Data encryption (b) Data integrity

   (c) Data deletion (d) Data replication

Ans: (b) Data integrity

2. Which cryptographic key is shared publicly in a blockchain network?

   (a) Private key (b) Public key

   (c) Symmetric key (d) Hash key

Ans: (b) Public key

3. What type of ledger does blockchain use?

   (a) Centralized ledger (b) Distributed ledger

   (c) Encrypted ledger (d) Sequential ledger

Ans: (b) Distributed ledger

Category-II *(Revised Bloom's Level-4, 5 & 6)*

1. Which privacy mechanism would you recommend to ensure anonymity while maintaining transaction transparency on a public blockchain?

   (a) Symmetric encryption (b) Zero-knowledge proofs

   (c) Digital signatures (d) Public key hashing

Ans: (b) Zero-knowledge proofs

2. Identify the most critical factor for balancing transparency and privacy in government-based blockchain applications:

   (a) Decentralization level (b) Cryptographic algorithms used

   (c) Consensus mechanism employed (d) Permissioned access control

Ans: (d) Permissioned access control

TEACHER'S KNOW MORE

- **Blockchain for Record-Keeping**: Teachers can use blockchain to securely manage academic records, e-transcripts, and certifications, ensuring transparency and immutability.
- **Smart Contracts in Education**: Automate course delivery, assignments, and progress tracking using blockchain-based smart contracts, reducing administrative workload.
- **Privacy and Security**: Learn how blockchain cryptography safeguards sensitive student data from unauthorized access and ensures data integrity.
- **Reward Systems**: Use blockchain to gamify learning by awarding digital tokens or cryptocurrency for student achievements, enhancing engagement.
- **Future-Ready Skills**: Equip students with blockchain knowledge for real-world applications in education, finance, and beyond, fostering innovation and critical thinking.